IS IT ALL RIGHT TO BE HUMAN?

....

WILL I EVER HAVE PEACE?

BY

CHUCK BURROUGHS

Chuck Burroughs

Nolan Kerr Press
Cincinnati, OH

Chuck Burroughs/Nolan Kerr Press
1325 Lance Ct.
Lebanon, OH 45036 USA
www.nolankerr.com

Publisher's Note: This is a work of non-fiction. Some names have been changed to protect confidentiality. This manuscript represents the opinions of the author and no one else.

Book Layout ©2017 BookDesignTemplates.com
Cover art by Rose O'Reilly Hoisington

Is It All Right to be Human?/Chuck Burroughs
ISBN 978-1-7333402-3-6
Contact Chuck Burroughs at info@chuckburroughs.net
Contact Nolan Kerr Press at info@nolankerr.com

TABLE OF CONTENTS

....

PROLOGUE

....

Do I have value?

My conscious mind says "yes," but my subconscious says "no."

Yet I choose to live, to fight the war, the battle within.

I have become a Dragon-slayer and you can do it too.

The sweet taste of success:

My accomplishments are ever before me.

I have accomplished the impossible.

My disability led to anxiety, which led to depression, which led to obsessive-compulsive disorder.

I was trying as hard as I could to find solutions by thinking and thinking.

There is no cure medically – only management for your depression and OCD.

I keep looking for the answers.

DEDICATION

....

I dedicate this book to all my mentors.

To my wife Gail Burroughs and our unconditional love for each other.

To my friends for life – Don and Mary Swagerty, for their humor, hunting and fishing, playing cards and just plain having fun.

To Charles Nielsen, a college professor. We talked for hours over meals, went hunting and fishing, played cards, and walked nature trails. He recommended books to read as we talked about church and theology.

To James Wade, pastor and counselor. His church was one I could attend, and it allowed me to give up wanting to be a minister and to accept my human sexuality.

To Wilma Perry, preacher, college professor and counselor. She helped me with decision-making, worked on cognitive therapy, on how to process information, and to be positive about myself.

To Larry Day, counselor. He let me know I was of value, a pearl of great value. He did not support harsh preaching.

To Kaiser-Permanente's counselors and other professionals.

And, to Robert Davis, Ph.D., one of the greatest counselors I ever had. He reinforced that I have great value and encouraged me to write my story. He asked me to counsel and give advice to some of his clientele.

WHAT READERS SAY ABOUT "IS IT ALL RIGHT TO BE HUMAN?"

....

"This book is a true story of a man who overcame physical, mental and emotional challenges to become a successful husband, father, employee and business owner. His search for success and a church that would accept and value him as he is makes a compelling, easy to read story. This book will help others on their life journey."

- *Gary Salyers, friend and retired elementary school principal*

"Inspirational read about a man who grew up in an abusive house with learning disabilities, depression and some forms of anxiety disorders. It depicts his lifelong struggles with his faith and church. A sure read for the younger generation dealing with similar problems. He shows the world there is such a thing as success for all those who face such life challenges."

- *Lisa Starr, neighbor*

"This book shows how one person who is born with a birth defect, and suffers from depression and OCD, can overcome these disabilities and live a very successful and happy life. It also shows that you don't have to be a perfectionist to succeed in life. I recommend this reading to anyone who suffers from mental issues or for any caretakers who are assisting someone with mental problems."

- *Mr. Gail Hanson, friend (no relation to Chuck's wife)*

"After reading Chuck's story, I am in awe that he survived to be a kind and loving family man and a generous human being willing to go out of his way to help others in need. I am also in awe of his wife, who emotionally supported him throughout decades of marriage and three children."

- *Carolyn Kramer, fellow alumnus, Franklin High School*

"I sure enjoyed Chuck's life journey and his intent to share that with others in hopes of impacting their lives. His life is rich with experiences that were hard and challenging but didn't completely derail him from passing on his hope to others."

- *Julia Letgers*

"My new name for Chuck Burroughs is 'Mr. Kindness of Happy Valley.'"

- *Rachel Janzen*

FOREWORD

....

One mid-summer day six years ago, a man walked into my office who has proved to be extraordinary. Very troubled, he had recently left a psychiatric inpatient facility with symptoms of severe depression and OCD, both of lifelong standing. At the time he was 71 years of age, married with three children, but estranged from his two adult daughters who had labeled him "evil." He had seen several therapists over his lifetime, most of them associated with the Christian Church, and had managed to control turbulent obsessions for a span of 50 years, including fear of knives, feces, women, and most of all, religious teachings to which he had been exposed as a child and young adult.

Chuck came across as earnest, and in evident psychic pain. He began with a description of his "blue baby" oxygen-deprived birth, bringing with him medical reports of subsequent dyslexia and a "processing disorder" in memory and comprehension. But it was largely a major depression that had caused him to be recently hospitalized and taken off a heavy dose of S.S.R.I. antidepressants which only worsened his despair and anguish. A new medley of prescription drugs was dispensed, but he abandoned them as well after another bad reaction. In the six years I have seen him, Chuck eschewed drugs totally, turning instead to psychotherapy to deal with his obsessive thoughts and depression. To do so required that he pay out of pocket since his HMO would not free him to use his Medicare coverage or "outsource" his treatment in memory and comprehension.

Chuck was hopeless of any progress as his recent encounters with psychiatric care had proved so damaging and fruitless. Illiterate through high school and two years of college, he was accepted in the latter because he was a good basketball player. Once there however, Chuck spoke the party line at church, resulting in "promotion" to be a Sunday school teacher as a solid fundamentalist Christian.

In the months of treatment that followed, it became clear to me that Chuck is a man whose issues derived from both organic and psychic sources, deeply embedded, with religious and spiritual themes of sin and self-punishment. Chuck's adaptation to life was a test of character involving his earliest and most impactful learning experiences, under the sway of a perfectionistic, sometimes brutal father, and the fundamentalist authority of an "infallible" church.

Some background. Chuck was the second of three boys. Their father excelled in work as a Civil engineer, builder and small business entrepreneur; these were choices that in time became Chuck's own. The boys got along well with each other under their tyrannical, demanding, obsessive-compulsive father, who was quick to blame and punish verbally and physically. Chuck recalls being knocked to the floor at age 12 because he had left the refrigerator door ajar. Beatings with a strap were commonplace. Nevertheless, Chuck's father taught him manual skills that became the basis for his later career. Despite his painful memories, he still holds his dad in high esteem, and has forgiven his severity.

He remembers his mother with deep warmth and gratitude. She loved him and provided a gentle, caring alternative. In fact, she helped him with his reading and processing difficulties by reading to him until he could remember assignments and acquired a basic understanding of written schoolwork. In spite of this, he was routinely held out of sports because of low grades, even though he excelled at them during junior high and high school.

Chuck felt it was his job to be a go-between for his parents in the hope of blunting his father's brutality toward his mother. At the age of 5, he observed them having a fight. Both were naked, and he was certain his mother was being assaulted. He now believes his father wanted intercourse. Eventually, in Chuck's early twenties, his father left his wife of 38 years and married another woman.

Religion. Chuck was deeply and permanently impressed as a child with tenets of the Christian Church, fundamentalist style. During Bible crusades he was eager to answer the "altar call" and did so to the point that he was counseled to stop. He believed without question in the literal interpretation of the Bible as the "inerrant word of God." These convictions were not challenged by him until years later.

As a middle-aged adult, Chuck found that his depression and recurrent unwanted thoughts became overwhelming. During this period, he began to question why prayer and strict adherence to religion did so little to comfort and assuage his self-doubt. As cracks in his belief system widened, he began to search for a more compatible worship atmosphere and began a 25-year-long search for the right fit in a church less dogmatic. His search was driven by episodes of intense depression and shame whenever he gave voice to the slightest doubt. Prompt rejection was often the result, to his mind. In the past two years this pattern recurred after a new pastor became insistent that he erred in being opposed to conventional theology. He is still searching, but also questioning.

Beginning in college, he progressed through a series of different counselors and gradually became more determined in pointing out to any who would listen, the many contradictions in their religious creed. At times this made him a *persona non grata*. In at least two cases he was actively shunned by some in the congregation. Such rejection caused even more torment and obsessive self-criticism since he still felt compelled to speak out his doubts. He felt this left him little choice but to quit one congregation after another as he tested ten or more churches. In Chuck's therapy much effort has been made to forestall his impulsive protests of growing skepticism. Socially he failed to recognize that keeping his contrary ideas to himself is often necessary when trying to "fit in" to any group.

At home with wife and children, Chuck was dominant and early created a role much like his father's, without the physical brutality. His devoted wife deferred to him most of the time, freely admitting her own fearfulness at making decisions. In time his daughters came to regard him a sinner since he was not observing the compliant "Christian" attitude he had taught them, labeling his religious doubts signs of an "evil" personality. Their older brother got along with Chuck without much trouble or complaint.

In later life Chuck has become more generous, giving and supportive of both his children and grandchildren. As an example, he and his wife lodged and sheltered a person in the family who had attempted suicide. That person was about 24 years of age and had a few years of college. Chuck and his wife were shocked with what was going on. That person had an alcohol problem, but was not an alcoholic. After a few months with grandparents, that person was able to refrain from drinking, accepted adult responsibilities and could hold down a job. That person began to live successfully and excelled in facing challenges. Chuck and Gail provided a safe place for the individual to live while recovering. Chuck did give advice as best as he could, knowing the pain that life can bring.

With 50 plus years of experience as a psychotherapist, I pondered why I was interested and supportive. Chuck dictated a rough account of his life to a computer in the effort to explain his spiritual journey. He thought it might ease some of his children's conflicts and they might forgive him for mistakes he made as their once hypercritical dad. He began to seek a wider audience within and outside the church, helping others who suffered from similar struggles. It is his earnest desire to help people like himself. Encounters with former Sunday school students lit a flame in him when they returned years later to thank him for having been a solace through their own religious doubts. He volunteered for and became the primary source of building repairs of his former churches, and then began to seek out strangers who seemed to need help.

An early riser, Chuck breakfasts at an open-all-night cafe where homeless people gather, buying meals and providing them with his company. He has found a knack for locating strangers in distress, helping them, especially with depression. Chuck has long since practiced a wide range of kind acts and charitable contributions outside or within his church congregations: helping youths learn to ski and buying them necessary equipment, or hosting frequent dinners for 10 to 16 people from his different churches, always preparing the main course himself.

At one point in the past year, Chuck responded to my request that he describe what he had learned that helped him cope with depression and OCD. He was willing and eager to present to a group of other patients with both conditions. I arranged for him to do so, and after speaking for over an hour he was met with rapt attention, many questions and much discussion. Those attending were moved and apparently aided. At that point I began to see the prospect of Chuck's possible healing influence with a wider audience. At the same time, he prepared a packet of self-help materials and distributed them to interested persons, both familiar and strangers. A key in his presentation that day which struck me was his practical application of nearly all the methods the psychotherapy community has to offer in treating these most difficult conditions without medication.

Another vital aspect of Chuck's remedial approach, that proved to me his readiness to expand upon his lessons of a lifetime, was the sheer hopefulness in his refusal to accept defeat for very long in the process of growing in his therapy. He has remained undaunted through many reversals and obstacles. Even at the darkest hour he kept true to the belief that he could find a solution.

If you've read this so far and are still awake, let me answer why I have gone on and considered it worth your time. Chuck and others both deserve and need a wider audience in their attempts to support those who suffer from prolonged depression and/or OCD, that most difficult of neuroses to treat.

Here is a man who has spent a lifetime in fierce combat with multiple mental issues, and who survived renewed and able to present the clearest exposition of the new approaches to OCD treatment available, such as the work of Professor Jeremy Schwartz at UCLA Medical School and those authors who furnished a glimpse of new methods in the magazine *Psychotherapy Newsletter*. These ideas have been put to good use in an articulate but folksy way by Chuck. Together we have sought an instrument to offer his legacy to others; a result of remarkable triumph over mental illness - with diligence and a hopeful assertion of personal courage in the face of long odds. Here is Chuck in his own words.

-    Robert Wm. Davis, Ph.D., A.B.P.P.

Retired Clinical Psychologist and Diplomate of the American Board of Professional Psychology and elected member of the American Academy of Clinical Psychology

INTRODUCTION

••

I am now 81 years old. I've dealt with loss in many areas of my life. For instance, some of my closest friends have died. Some are still alive but suffer from mobility problems, so they don't get around much anymore. I was forced to retire my business due to my age and health problems. I can no longer snow ski, a favorite pastime of mine for 40 years. I can't even go bowling anymore. And the last church I belonged to turned me off with the pastor's use of sermons to project her personal political ideas. I don't think church is a place for politics of any kind.

You have probably heard stories about how isolation can reduce the quality of life for seniors. I have tried hard to keep myself active, walking four miles, five to six days a week. I walk with my dog in a lovely park in Happy Valley Oregon, and meet lots of people, some young and some not-so-young. As someone walks toward me, my dog and I step off the path; I bow to them, and say something like "I wish you well", or "I wish for you a good life." Sometimes, the person will say something in return, and we'll start a conversation; sometimes they look at me oddly and walk on by. Sometimes, if a connection is made, I invite them to my home for tea, and occasionally they accept. My wife Gail loves meeting new people and doesn't mind fixing refreshments during these visits.

As you will read in this book, I have suffered my whole life with learning disorders and also with mental health issues. I chose to learn about these ailments and to fight them, and never give up. I have read many books, and talked to many counselors, and gradually I learned about ways to overcome or at least compensate for my disabilities. In the process, I've learned to live a full and happy life.

My situation is more fortunate than many. I am now close to my children and grandchildren, and when they need financial support, I am able to help them. I feel very sad for young people who cannot afford to live independently, or attend college, or buy a car, or who have no close family to help them.

Before the COVID pandemic started, Oregon had the third-highest suicide rate in the US. I believe there are many reasons for this. Some people are hounded by addiction to drugs or alcohol. Others are barely able to keep themselves in food and shelter because they cannot find or keep a job. Others are just plain lonely. I like to think that when I start a conversation with someone in the park, I am helping to make them a little less lonely. I know it works for me.

I've written a list of 34 things that have helped me to cope with my disabilities. They are included in this book. I have also included a list of books that have helped me overcome depression and anxiety problems related to my Obsessive-Compulsive Disorder.

When I walk in the park in Happy Valley, I always bring along packets of my lists and suggestions for people I might meet. I never know when a person I speak with will be someone struggling with depression or other issues. I ask them if they would like one of my packets, and if they say yes, I give them one. The rest is up to God. Occasionally, I will see those people again on another of my walks in the park, and they will tell me how my packet helped them. That is the best feeling.

What follows in this book is the story of my life: how I was born and raised; my struggles with a fundamentalist church doctrine that contributed to my illness; and how, with the help of many, I married, raised a family, built a successful business; and finally, turned my experiences into power for others struggling with similar problems as mine. Whether or not you are one who suffers from any of these issues I describe, I hope you will find inspiration to live your best life in these pages.

-   *Chuck Burroughs*

PART ONE: MY FAMILY STORY

••

CHAPTER ONE: VIVID MEMORIES OF MY PARENTS

....

The easiest, quickest way to communicate is simply to say something and then hear the other person's reply, right? Right, unless your listener has a CAPD (Central Auditory Processing Disorder). Then, your remarks might come through with certain words drowned out by other noises, or with some words sounding like different words or as a meaningless string of verbiage. People with CAPDs (usually part of a learning disability) have been embarrassed by situations like these all their lives. A language processing disorder (LPD) is an impairment that negatively affects communication through spoken language. There are two types of LPD—people with expressive language disorder have trouble expressing thoughts clearly, while those with receptive language disorder have difficulty understanding others.

One person with a language disorder might find it difficult to speak extemporaneously or outline what they are thinking, while another person might struggle to understand what others are saying, to follow directions, or to maintain attention.

You know the feeling: You're in the middle of telling a great story when suddenly the word you're looking for gets stuck "on the tip of your tongue." Or you're 10 minutes into a conversation before you realize you haven't taken in a word the other person is saying. For most people, these brief mental slipups can be annoying, but for someone with an expressive or receptive language disorder, they can be a constant reality. And the cumulative effect of a lifetime of communication difficulties can be devastating.

- *Judith W. Paton, M.A., "Living and Working with a Central Auditory Processing Disorder"*

My full name is Charles Daniel Burroughs. I was born on August 2, 1939 at 126 Warren Avenue, Franklin, Ohio. My father was Roy Burroughs, and my mother was Virginia Doty Burroughs. Our family doctor, for over 40 years, was there to help with my birth. There was a rumor that the day I was born that the doctor was drunk. I don't know whether that was true.

I was raised mostly in Franklin, Ohio, which is between Dayton and Cincinnati. There was a problem with my birth. The umbilical cord was wrapped around my neck, shutting off oxygen to my brain. There was nothing anyone could do. I had some damage to a portion of my brain. It affected my ability to process information, and to learn how to read, write, spell and pronounce words. Comprehending things in sequence is very difficult – such as taking directions to a location and remembering what was said, and in what order the directions were given.

I believe several things in my early years contributed to some of the challenges I ended up facing throughout my life.

A warning - there are things in here that may be hard for one to read. But I believe it is the truth. I faced four major difficulties in life. First, I was born with a handicap. Second, my parents were very dysfunctional and toxic in their raising of me and my brothers. Dad came from extreme hardship, and it was remarkable on his part to overcome many of those difficulties. Third, I believe my dad's mother was mentally ill with depression - which she likely inherited and passed on to her grandchildren, especially me and my brother Denny. Of course, it could show up in future generations. Hopefully it will not. I think everybody, at some time in life, suffers with depression, and this is normal. I say to my grandchildren - don't worry about it. Just remember that your Grandpa Chuck rose above some very severe depression. I want you to realize how hard I worked to overcome these obstacles. I believe at times God surely had His hand upon me. That, plus a lot of good people really helped me.

My father. Just who was my father, Roy Burroughs? I was named after his father – Charles. My grandfather Charles was very poor. His job was delivering ice and oil for lamps. My dad's mother was never talked about. As I remember, the only thing I knew was that she was institutionalized.

My father was a rigid dictator. He controlled everything in my childhood. His greatest fear was that he would not succeed in making a good living. This made him controlling; he treated my mother like he owned her and always had to tell her what to do. She couldn't buy a potato without his permission.

My parents had three children, all boys. I was the middle one. My father used guilt and shame to manage us. He never gave us praise or acceptance. He seemed to look upon me as costing him money. It seemed money and succeeding in business were the most important things to him.

As a child, my dad Roy often went to bed hungry. Sometimes, we were told, my Aunt Bessie helped raise my dad. As far as I know, my dad took over responsibility for his dad at a very young age. In high school my dad earned a scholarship from the Lions Club, and then went off to college and became a civil engineer. My dad said he felt so guilty about leaving his father and mother to go to college. I'm not sure when electricity came to the homes for light and refrigeration, but it put his dad out of work. I can only imagine what life was like for dad and his father with very little income.

When dad graduated from college, he bought the home on Warren Ave. My dad was very tight-lipped and didn't talk about his family. Therefore, I know very little about my grandmother or my grandfather. I do remember that my dad put a trailer in the backyard on Warren, where my grandfather lived. Grandpa would invite us into his trailer to show me a monkey in the mirror and we all laughed. The only other thing that my dad said about his dad, was that he didn't appreciate him until he died. It was like my father was ashamed of his family and of his heritage. My dad told us, in a letter to me and my brothers, Mike and Denny, about his mother. My dad was dying of lung cancer from smoking. His exact words: "My mother became a mental patient: she left my dad, roamed the streets, and ended up in a mental institution." No one in the family could understand. This is all that my dad said about his mother, my grandmother, and that is all I know.

Hating the silence. My dad really knew how to build and repair things. He was a problem solver. He had had experience doing without. However, there was no talking about feelings or emotions in our house. I grew up hating the silence about what was happening in our lives. I always felt guilty because I never got approval, never felt accepted by my father. He had one goal to achieve, a middle class or higher economic status, so he was extremely ambitious. Work was his way of life.

This had to come from his parents. However, my dad was like a rooster who did things his way and always said he was right. He didn't have many friends. He did very little talking about the past. Everything about family and money seemed to me to be a secret. He did have a strong work ethic. We didn't talk about life issues or religion. However, he did pass on strong ethics, honesty and integrity. He said, when you work for someone, you give your absolute best.

Through his work my dad accomplished many things. He did survey work, which is finding property owners' legal boundaries, and that required a license. He had to file and record records, draw up plat drawings of boundaries. After a time in Arkansas where my brother Mike was born, he worked for McGraw Construction Company, then later in Butler, Pennsylvania, laying out railroad tracks. While doing his survey work, he ran a paint and wallpaper store and a restaurant. He also built apartments in Franklin, Ohio. This was in the 1960s. That was when I started thinking about building apartments.

My dad set a good example as an entrepreneur and being financially successful. He laid the foundation for me to become a contractor. I learned from him how to paint and roof a house, pour concrete and build an addition onto a house. He helped me get jobs as a teenager. I became a carpenter's helper and worked with brick layers one summer. By age 15, I had the foundation to be a contractor, which was my profession for much of the rest of my life.

My dad the surveyor. My dad got involved with the city of Franklin due to his abilities as a surveyor. There was a major highway running to Dayton, Ohio, and also south to Cincinnati. There were no freeways at that time. There was a large hill rising from that road where someone wanted to build a house. The developer was seeking approval from the city of Franklin. On the other side of the road was an old canal that had been abandoned. This canal ran short distances north and south, parallel to the road. The question was, if you put in roads and housing, when it rained would the water runoff cross the road and flood the housing adjacent to the road? It happened to be a block away from where we lived. Our good friend lived next to the road. The city approved the plans and let the builder start building this new subdivision. My father was against this development. He said that there would be a lot of water that would flood the housing below, and of course, that is exactly what happened to our street on Warren Avenue. The water ran into the basements and it made things bad for those houses. Oh my, I was so proud of my father. He knew what he was doing. The city, I think, came in and dug the canal deeper and also improved the storm sewers that had to be enlarged to handle the water. I don't know who paid the bill. The builder was a very good house builder and an entrepreneur in his field. As I would realize in later years, there is always big risk when you are an entrepreneur.

My dad's physical stature was small, but he always let you know he was the boss, very much in control of everything. If he wasn't, he used his tongue and his words to put you in your place. I admit that I hated my dad when I was young, and on into my 30s. But I forgave my father because I went back through what I knew about him and tried to understand what life was like for him, what his goals were, what his fears were. He was afraid of failure and poverty. He was raised in poverty, so he thought he had to make all the decisions about everything for our family. His business was to fight everybody for control, or so he thought. By doing this, he and others would be successful. What he didn't know was the great harm he was doing to his children, his wife, and the people who tried to be his friend. Many of us resented him. He also talked very harshly, even to our mother. Unfortunately, this caused trouble later in our lives with our wives and friends. I think my dad thought that feelings, emotions - certainly crying - were weaknesses. And he wasn't going to be weak, so these emotions never showed. He never expressed acceptance to his children. He never spoke words of love. It seems if you were perfect in your work, he thought this would bring success. You couldn't play or have fun. It seemed this was the way it was. This sounds extreme, but that seemed to be the total message: work, work, and more work.

I remember being told when I went off to college that he ran down to the basement crying. He had to hide himself because a man doesn't show emotion, feelings, or express love. I think my brother Mike would see it a little differently. I think the first child in the family takes the brunt of the harshness more. Maybe my dad eased up when the third child came along.

I have tried my best to grow socially and understand what it means to be a man. I resented the movies made by John Wayne for how he talked to women and those around him. I had to work on talking differently, but sometimes it comes blurting out.

My older brother Denny would make harsher statements of hatred towards my father. My younger brother Mike would say nice things about our father. I have forgiven my father, and I think Mike also has forgiven him, but Denny never did.

When I would go to my father for help, in trying to find answers, or trying to solve a problem at a very young age, it was a nightmare for me. He made it so difficult. I always felt miserable because he was a perfectionist and demanded that I make no mistakes. And, of course, with my disability, I would rarely go to him for help. My father did teach that a man must know everything and be right about everything, and be perfect about everything, and of course this caused me great emotional harm. It was my mother who brought comfort, protection and reason to my life.

The warmth of Aunt Bessie. Aunt Bessie was an editor and writer for a newspaper in West Virginia. Our family spent some time with her at a cabin next to a river, and boated and fished. However, I must have done something wrong once and had been sent upstairs to bed without supper. I was really broken and crying. And Bessie came into my bedroom and told me my dad was totally wrong and I was a good little boy. Oh how I felt vindicated and restored – but I hated my dad, nothing new, that's the way it was. At eighty-one years old I can still hear those wonderful words: I am a good little boy.

My dad introduced me to boating. He had a wooden boat about 16 feet long with a 25-horsepower motor. We lived next to the Great Miami River. I don't remember using the boat much with my dad, but when I was teenager, Denny and I used the boat on rivers and lakes. I can remember driving to a lake in Ohio, and dad rented a cabin. We spent a week there fishing and boating. I loved it. This was one of the great times in our lives.

Hunting became a passion for me. Dad took us pheasant and rabbit hunting in Ohio. I remember him teaching me to be cautious about hunting, how to carry a gun, and how to cross a fence. It seemed to me that I did something special harvesting pheasants and rabbits that brought my dad pleasure or happiness because I did it well. I didn't want to hunt on my own, just with my dad. Mom loved cooking rabbits and pheasants. Our family had a feast at these times.

When I was 13, my dad owned a restaurant business he ran in a rented building. In that type of business, the waitresses are a big part of how well financially you do. As you must know by now, my dad was not good working with people. He always disliked waitresses after he sold the business. I don't know if the restaurant was a failure financially. I just know he owned it for a while, then he didn't anymore. He was certainly an entrepreneur, seeking and trying new things to make money. However, I remember, as a young adult, going out to eat at a restaurant. My father would embarrass me and others with his harsh words with all waitresses. He would pick a fight with them about anything. I always resented having him pay for our meals. My father loved to take us out to eat a meal with him. This felt like success to him because of his living in poverty and going to bed hungry. Eating out embodied the fruits of victory and success, and of course, who doesn't like going out and eating? This was a pleasure for our family most of the time, if the waitresses handled our dad with kid gloves.

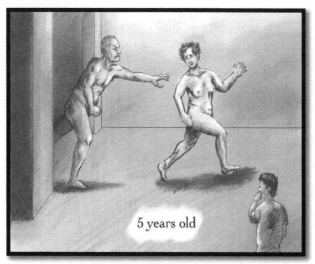

5 years old

Lasting memories about my father and sex A disturbing story about my dad and mother and me: I was probably 4 years old, maybe five or six, I don't remember exactly. This event was to have a huge effect on my life in a negative way. I was in the living room and I could hear a fight going on. I could hear mother and dad yelling argumentative words to one another. I could hear physical banging around. I heard noises - someone falling out of bed onto the floor - there was a big bang. I could hear crying. Mother ran out from the bedroom. Mother was naked, dad was naked, and mother was crying and crying. What could I do? It was obvious dad was beating up on mother. I wanted to protect her. I wanted to beat up dad, but I was helpless in trying to protect my mother. Dad ran forward and told me to go outside and play. What could I do? I did it. I went outside. That was the beginning of, or maybe continuation of, my hatred towards my father. They say children learn from the example set by their parents. We learn how to be sexual beings. This had a profound effect on me for the rest of my life. I denied that I was a sexual person. I wasn't going to be like dad. Sex was hurtful for the woman, so I pushed those feelings deep inside of me.

My dad, at 53 years of age, was taking a night course at a college in Ohio and had a major heart attack. Fortunately for him, there was a doctor there that gave him the necessary first aid and then transported dad to a hospital. I saw him the next day, and dad was blue in the face, in critical condition, but he did fully recover from his heart attack. It took him a year to recover.

My father built apartments in Franklin, Ohio and also bought a house on Main Street. After I went off to college in Oregon, my dad sold the Warren Ave. house and moved into the apartments.

Mother, I think, was broken. Her children had left the nest, and she was in a difficult marriage. She was a typical woman of that time whose husband made all the decisions, and she had no say. I think she started saying what she wanted. However, it was too late, in my opinion. Dad divorced mother and married Opal, a very nice lady who could hold her own with dad in some ways. My father paid my mother off, splitting, I think, half of their assets.

My dad's lung cancer took him at age 80. At his funeral I said nice things about him. As an adult, I understood that he was truly an unusual man, living in poverty, getting a college degree and becoming an entrepreneur. He made lots of mistakes. I know he felt guilty about divorcing mother. He, however, didn't have a clue why his children, Denny and Chuck, suffered with emotional problems. I cannot speak for Mike, though I think he did too.

The refrigerator door. A particular incident happened when I was a teenager in Ohio. It was extremely hot and humid during the summer, especially August. You would take a shower, dry off, and within minutes you were sweating again, wringing wet. One day I went to the refrigerator to get a cool drink. I walked across the floor to the counter to pour my drink into a glass. I made a big mistake. I left the refrigerator door open. My dad came into the kitchen, and immediately knocked me to the floor with angry words about him paying the bills and I was terribly wrong to leave the refrigerator door open. It came as a total shock to me. Oh, I wanted to hit him in the worst way. To this day, sometimes I leave the refrigerator door open and I say to myself - "you can't beat me up today, I can leave the refrigerator door open if I choose to do so." Then, the memories of how awful I was treated by my father come back to me.

The beatings that I took from my father at times seemed extremely inappropriate and harsh. He had a wide leather belt that he would use so many times. He thought he was helping us by strapping us. I can remember being 14 or 15 years old, taking that belt and burning it up in the back yard. He never knew where that belt went. Hurray for me! Taking action against brutality.

I had the feeling that my dad was so into making money and saving wherever he could, that he saw his children as taking away his money. There must have been a war going on inside him, between loving his family and seeing us as valuable, and not a burden on his pocketbook.

My mother. It is hard to remember a great deal about my mother because I was spending all my energy trying to defend myself against my father's verbal abuse, which made me feel shamed and guilt-ridden. However, I owe much to my mother as she was the one to help me get through school. I loved my mother dearly, appreciating her love of me.

My mom, Virginia, ran off and eloped with my father Roy, and they were married by a justice of the peace. My mother was very good-looking and had a very outstanding figure when she was young. My mother was quiet and silent. She became a beautician and loved working to make women beautiful. She was from a large family. Her mother married three times and buried three husbands. My mother's brothers were Joe, Eston and Aaron. She had a sister who was adopted, named Jerry. I'm not sure what her maiden name was.

My mother was a kind, patient, and loving woman. She loved to wait on her family, hand and foot. We always had clean clothing and she kept the house very clean. She cooked wonderful meals. However, the meals of that time were lots of meat, Crisco oil, potatoes, gravy and a few vegetables. This was unhealthy cooking by our standards today. This was what my mother taught me to cook. I can remember baking a cake or cookies, and mother would give us the spoon to lick, or the bowl of chocolate. How wonderful this was.

With three boys in the family, we used to get milk delivered to our house in large, heavy crates. We drank milk like it was the only thing to drink. We consumed large quantities. One day, mother went out and picked up a heavy crate of milk and hurt her back severely. What do you do when you get hurt? Back then you went to bed and stayed there until you got better. I remember them placing a board underneath the cushion on the couch in the living room, where she laid all day. Nowadays, you would do that, but you would stretch and exercise the back muscles to strengthen them, and not lay in bed. They did a lot of things back then that made things worse, not better. I became the family cook, and I loved it. Of course, mother helped me and encouraged me.

Mother was a peacemaker, the protector, and the problem solver with the family issues. Mother read my schoolbooks to me all through grade school and high school and we used flashcards to learn the alphabet and mathematics. Many a late night in the kitchen, she worked with me. Of course, we didn't know that I was born with a processing disorder, both visual and hearing. But I think, because she read my schoolbooks to me, I was able to get a high school education. I picked up a lot from her.

Unfortunate use of the belt. My mother did occasionally use the belt strap also. There was one time when I was nine or ten years old and I was sitting on the pot doing my business, number two, and I must've done something wrong. She went and got the belt. I ran to the living room. I was facing her, and she hit me with that belt, and it landed across my penis. I screamed and screamed. She was shocked and I know she felt terrible. That had some effect on me going to the bathroom. It was like I was ashamed of myself having to go, for being a human being. This did affect me the rest of my life. I know she spanked me for a reason. I never knew the reason why; was it because I was going to the toilet? I don't know what I was getting spanked for. It certainly was a mistake on her part not to make it clear why I was getting spanked.

Mother started a Cub Scout troop, where a number of boys would gather at our house. She had a helper, but I don't remember much about that time. I do remember feeling good about doing Boy Scout things. I was so proud of my mother for doing this in our neighborhood. It seemed to me that my parents were leaders within their circle of friends.

Halloween was a big deal at our house, and my friends loved to come to our house because my mother made popcorn balls. She had a special recipe for making delicious, sweet popcorn balls. The neighbors loved coming in and getting the special treat every year. At those times, I felt my parents were the greatest and could do no harm.

Christmas was a huge celebration, with Santa Claus and lots and lots of toys. When dad had the paint and wallpaper store where he also sold toys, this meant that we three boys got many, many toys. The Christmas tree was a big deal. It was so beautiful with the lights. I used to sit at night and stare at the Christmas tree in wonder. That was a beautiful, exciting time. I do think the hype was too great. I always had a big letdown after Christmas. We really received way too many things. I wanted dad and mom to spend time with me, talk to me, and not give me material things. And so much silence - no time for talking or playing or for having fun. It was work, more work, and more work. Our work was never done.

Thanksgiving also was a wonderful time, with mother's relatives coming to our house for dinner. I don't know whether this started my love of gatherings with family and friends for dinners or not, but it was a big deal. This is where I learned to love turkey, mashed potatoes, and gravy. Oh, how heavenly these meals were. One Thanksgiving, one of mother's brothers wouldn't come to our house. There was a big rift between Aaron Doty and my father. It had a long-term effect on the family, Aaron's children and me, Mike and Denny. This one was not necessarily my father's fault.

Mother and dad. I often felt sorry for my mother. In trying to keep peace between my parents, I stayed neutral, not taking sides, but at the same time hating my father for abusing her. I tried to play peacemaker to make my father happy, which was impossible. Dad, the banty rooster, was always going in different directions. He fought with his peers, using unfair words to get his way by putting down those around him. Mother, somehow, took his verbal and sometimes physical abuse. Once, when I was a teenager, my father lost his job, and a fight broke out between my mother and dad. Unusual for me, I took Dad's side. Mother called me a traitor. This hurt me, but I knew she didn't mean it.

One more story about dad and mom fighting, and my wishing things could be different. A vacuum cleaner salesman came to the house, and mother was impressed with this vacuum cleaner. She wanted to buy it, but dad did not want to buy this particular vacuum cleaner. There was a large battle between the two. I wanted to buy the vacuum cleaner and put dad in his place. However, I was just a kid. I couldn't do anything to help mom, so the vacuum cleaner guy was sent packing. But my dad went out to a store and bought a new vacuum cleaner and gave it to mom to use. Mom probably hated that vacuum cleaner, but that's the way it was.

A dog and a vacation. One year, we all took a trip to Washington, D.C. to see the Capitol of the United States, and then went to visit Niagara Falls. It must've been August, and terribly hot and humid. My parents decided to take this trip, except they were fighting like cats and dogs. How was I going to bring peace to this situation? Dad insisted on bringing our Fox Terrier dog with us on the trip. Mother wanted to put the dog in a kennel. Again, dad had to be in control and show everybody that he knew best. Oh my, what a mess this was. They fought and made the trip miserable for all of us. There was nothing I could do but try to make the best of it and enjoy the trip. I did enjoy Washington, D.C., especially the statue of Abraham Lincoln. There was something about his statue, and what we knew from history classes about Abraham Lincoln. And yes, I enjoyed seeing the Niagara Falls, staying in motels and eating out; but there was this barking, scrapping dog. I love dogs, but mother was right, dad was wrong. Why couldn't these two bring peace to our family and do the right thing? Of course, I loved the dog. But the heat of those hot, humid summer days made things even more miserable.

After my parents divorced, my mother felt lost. She struggled financially even though she worked at an ice cream parlor for a few years in Cincinnati. My younger brother Mike took care of her because by then I was living in Oregon. I always felt guilty that I was not there to help her.

My mother passed away at age 76 from cancer. She was my role model.

CHAPTER TWO: MY BROTHERS, DENNY AND MIKE

•••

Dyslexia refers to a cluster of symptoms that result in difficulties with specific language skills, particularly reading. Students with dyslexia often experience difficulties with both oral and written language skills, such as writing and pronouncing words. Dyslexia affects individuals throughout their lives; however, its impact can change at different stages in a person's life. It is referred to as a learning disability because dyslexia can make it very difficult for a student to succeed without phonics-based reading instruction that is unavailable in most public schools. In its more severe forms, a student with dyslexia may qualify for special education with specially designed instruction, and as appropriate, accommodations.

The exact causes of dyslexia are still not completely clear, but anatomical and brain imagery studies show differences in the way the brain of a person with dyslexia develops and functions. Moreover, most people with dyslexia have been found to have difficulty with identifying the separate speech sounds within a word and/or learning how letters represent those sounds, a key factor in their reading difficulties. Dyslexia is not due to either lack of intelligence or desire to learn; with appropriate teaching methods, individuals with dyslexia can learn successfully.

The impact that dyslexia has is different for each person and depends on the severity of the condition and the effectiveness of instruction or remediation. The core difficulty is with reading words and this is related to difficulty with processing and manipulating sounds. Some individuals with dyslexia manage to learn early reading and spelling tasks, especially with excellent instruction, but later experience their most challenging problems when more complex language skills are required, such as grammar, understanding textbook material, and writing essays.

People with dyslexia can also have problems with spoken language, even after they have been exposed to good language models in their homes and good language instruction in school. They may find it difficult to express themselves clearly, or to fully comprehend what others mean when they speak. Such language problems are often difficult to recognize, but they can lead to major problems in school, in the workplace, and in relating to other people. The effects of dyslexia can reach well beyond the classroom.

Dyslexia can also affect a person's self-image. Students with dyslexia often end up feeling less intelligent and less capable than they actually are. After experiencing a great deal of stress due to academic problems, a student may become discouraged about continuing in school.

- *International Dyslexia Association*

My brother Denny. Denny graduated from high school and attended college for two years. My dad insisted on my brother Denny going to college and becoming a civil engineer. This was not good from Denny's point of view. He had some kind of learning disability also, perhaps dyslexia. The principal came to dad and mom and said that he was concerned that there was something wrong with Denny. Denny didn't seem to understand teachers telling him to do something. Denny didn't follow instructions well at a young age. It seemed that Denny didn't want to become a civil engineer. Eventually he dropped out and became an assistant to tax assessors, then joined the military.

Denny joined the Seventh Cavalry of the Armed Forces and was sent to Korea. Denny came home with a medical discharge after a few years and returned to live with dad and mom. His struggle with mental illness started to become apparent. He checked himself into a Veterans hospital, and stayed there for three or four months, before going back home. The Veterans Hospital only made things worse.

I have talked to my brother Denny about his experiences with our father. You see, he was four years older than I am. Denny lived in Cincinnati. To Denny's credit, he handled his mental illness. He didn't commit suicide but toughed it out. He called it climbing the mountain. He said, near the end of his life, that he was at the top.

Denny said that, while he wasn't sure, he thought our dad's mother was mentally ill, and that she slept with many men. When we lived on Warren Ave., Dad's mother came to the house and asked if dad would take her in and take care of her. Denny was present, and heard dad say no, with good reason. So, my dad placed her in some kind of home; it could have been a place for the mentally ill. Dad probably paid the bills. We don't know how this was worked out.

Denny said that dad was a womanizer who drank in bars where he would pick up women. Denny said that one time dad came home and asked our mother for a divorce. He wanted to live with another woman. Mother told him she would grant the divorce, if he took the three boys. Dad went back to the woman and told her. The woman told dad to go to hell.

I can remember another one of these womanizing times. I thought that dad had a pretty blonde he was seeing. Mother went to the pastor and asked for help and counsel. Dad gave up the blonde.

Denny also said mother, at one time, talked about committing suicide, taking Denny into the kitchen and lying on the floor, turning on the gas stove to asphyxiate them both. Denny told mom, "We can't do this." And mom didn't carry out what she started.

During this time, dad was recovering from his heart attack, and had very little income. Dad tried to do survey work, but could not do it on his own. Denny started helping dad do the survey work. Also, Denny said that dad's ability to think clearly had declined. Denny would stay by his side, assisting dad with meetings, with reading plat drawings, and land surveys, while dad met with potential customers. Denny assisted dad in landing those jobs. However, Denny was in a downward slide, withdrawing from people. They were two wounded people, helping one another.

My wife Gail and I visited dad and mother during the Christmas of 1962. We remember Denny living in the basement like a hermit and totally withdrawing from society. Only later, probably two years or so, he went to work for Goodwill. This was going to be a long, long road for Denny to be able to function in society and take care of himself. But he made it. He married a woman named Bernice who was also working at Goodwill. She had a bipolar disorder. Denny and Bernice managed apartments for many years. Denny also became a security guard.

Denny Burroughs passed away on Christmas Day in 2018 at the age of 83. Denny had a military funeral and was cremated and placed in the cemetery where his wife was buried.

I traveled back to Ohio and my brother Mike and his wife Shirley paid for me to stay in a nice hotel which I thoroughly enjoyed. My son Tim traveled with me. I asked for a tour of Cincinnati to see all the outstanding places the city is known for. It was a great time for family to see each other and have long talks about life. Being a religious family of various degrees, we shared our mutual love for God and our differences in theology.

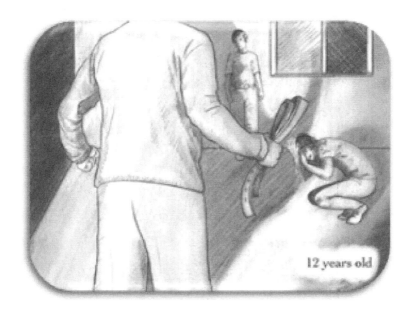

12 years old

Denny and me at the golf course. One night Denny and I, then in our teens, climbed out the back bedroom windows and went to the Franklin golf course. We just ran around having a ball. This was late at night. We thought mom and dad were asleep and we could sneak back and climb in the windows, and they wouldn't know that we were gone. Of course, things didn't work out as we'd hoped. We hiked back to our house and got caught climbing in the windows. Dad was furious and the belt came out. Denny was beaten and I received some licks also, but Denny got the worst of it. Again, dad punished us in a severe way. Naturally, I thought dad was awful. I felt so sorry for Denny. We didn't do anything that terrible, but that's not what dad thought.

I struggled with what to say at Denny's memorial service, because he had struggled with mental illness most of his adult life. However, he managed this illness pretty well. I gave praise to the family that lived in Cincinnati for helping him cope and manage his illness. Life is a struggle and there is negative heartache thinking of what his life could have been but wasn't. He managed apartments, he was a security guard, and he was in the military in Korea. He got a medical discharge which entitled him to a monthly income. He got married. As the years went by and his health deteriorated, he became a hermit, relying on Todd Burroughs, my brother Mike's son, to take care of him. I praise the family, because Denny could very easily have committed suicide if it had not been for the support that each family member gave him.

My brother Mike. My brother Mike is four years younger than I am. I really don't remember much about our childhood together. Denny and I lived and slept in the same bedroom and Denny and I were quite involved in doing things together. While Mike was part of the family, I really didn't do much with Mike. Since we became adults, he has shown great respect for me and we have spent some time together when we could. We have shared our lives in an open way by phone. Mike has come to stay with us in our homes at different times for a visit. And I've gone to Cincinnati to visit him. Mike and I also hunted pheasant together on various occasions over the years.

At times Mike and I have given advice to one another about life, religion and money. Because of Mike's college education and the fact that he runs a mortgage company, I have looked to Mike for advice on buying homes and dealing with family members, who have needed advice on money problems. How should I invest in the stock market? Should I do a reverse mortgage? My respect and love for Mike and his wife Shirley and his children and grandchildren has continued to grow over the years.

CHAPTER THREE: GROWING UP

···

It takes specialized testing to identify a Central Auditory Processing Disorder (CAPD.) These include tests of auditory memory, sequencing, tonal pattern recognition or sound blending, and storing of general information. The most accurate way to sort out CAPDs from other problems is through clinical audiologic tests of central nervous system function. If a therapist finds that your child has a language disorder, she will work with you to set up a treatment plan, which usually includes speech therapy. If the language disorder has negatively affected the patient's social and academic growth in dramatic ways — which is more likely the older they are at the time of diagnosis — it's possible that psychotherapy will be recommended as well. If a language disorder isn't caught early or is misdiagnosed, it can create wide-reaching complications in a person's life — complications that often extend from childhood to adulthood. Social situations, for example, can be challenging for someone with either a receptive or an expressive language disorder. Difficulties with self-expression or with comprehension of what others are saying can cause someone to withdraw or endure being ostracized.

-   Judith Paton, M.A., WebMD

I was named after my grandfather, Charles. For a short time, my grandfather lived with us, so as not to confuse us, my parents gave me a new name, Tad. I liked it when I was growing up in Franklin. However, when I moved to Oregon, I asked people to call me Chuck. Everybody in Ohio called me Tad, but in Oregon they call me Chuck.

When I was born in the late 1930s, it was always cold in the winter with lots of snow, and extremely hot and humid in the summer. I can remember the old coal furnace where dad would have to start the fire early in the mornings. These furnaces were called octopuses because of the large duct work in the basement. There was a room just for storing coal. The coal delivery truck would pull up in our driveway and shovel coal into a coal chute. The coal would slide into that room. I can remember getting up those cold mornings and standing in the kitchen. Mother would open the oven, and we would warm ourselves in front of the stove. At the time, I didn't realize that coal was the best way to heat the house. While modern then, today it seems very antiquated.

The house seemed so big at that time. It was only a three-bedroom home. My toys were soldiers, tanks, trucks, and marbles. We were fighting in World War II, so soldier toys were what kids played with. There must've been lots of fear. Mother, later in my life, seemed afraid. Of course I didn't understand, but I sensed something was wrong. Probably it was her marriage and the war. This was not to say that mother didn't love our dad, because she did. I think she loved him very deeply.

I started having nightmares, or dreams of German paratroopers jumping out of planes and coming to kill us. In my dreams, it was up to me to save the family. Where to hide, what was I going to do? I had a gun, and I tried my best to kill those Germans - and then I would wake up. These dreams started at around six or eight years old. I was in my 20s before they stopped.

School. School back then didn't have a Head Start program. Maybe they had kindergarten, but I don't remember. I remember first grade, second grade, and third grade. I remember the alphabet letters as upside down and backwards; that's how they looked to me. I remember being scolded by teachers. My nightmare with school had started. However, there was a principal who came into class and pulled me out one day. He gave me a screwdriver and asked me to fix a piece of metal stripping that had come loose from the concrete floor. I remember working and working on this, but couldn't fix it, though I tried so hard. This became such a wonderful thing for me. I loved it, trying to fix something. This was a huge clue to the work I would do as a contractor later in life.

In school they set me back two years, as I still couldn't read well. My parents hired a tutor for me. I worked as hard as I could, but I still didn't get it. There were other students who had trouble reading, but their tutors performed miracles for them. They learned to read and write, but I couldn't. Oh my, what a nightmare. Sometimes, the teachers would call on me to read, especially substitute teachers who didn't know me. I could not. I had a way of being very aggressive in class, in a good way, so they would call on me to read and I couldn't. I remember daydreaming a lot, looking out the windows to pass the time. At night my mother would read my books to me. Oh, if the teachers had just given me an oral test I could have passed. I believed this, but they didn't, and I suffered.

In grades four, five and six, sports became a big deal in my life - baseball, flag football and some basketball. All this was heavenly for my life.

It was during this time, when I was around 13, that my dad owned the restaurant. At noon, I would hike down to his restaurant and eat my lunch, then get a big ice cream cone with many, many, many scoops. There wasn't much time to get there and get back to school in time. I think it had to be one hour. One day the principal called me into his office. He asked me what the teachers were doing to help me, because there was another student who couldn't read or write. I must have made a little progress, for him to ask me. I didn't know what to say because I didn't feel I was doing very well. I felt terrible about myself, so he sent me back. I felt, man, I wish I could have helped, but I didn't.

During my grade school years, it seemed to me that I wanted, in the worst way, to be a leader, to be assertive. I was always trying to do that with my peers, but my lack of reading and writing skills was always my downfall. I felt like I was a failure and I tried not to think about it. I also was big in size, and there was always someone who picked fights with me because I was two years older than the other kids in my class. I was the person to beat up to prove they were better than me. This was a problem throughout my school years, through high school. That's the way it was.

What I loved to do. Basketball became big in my life. On Saturdays they had basketball at the big high school for us grade school kids. They started teaching us different skills, dribbling, shooting the ball, running, passing - and we got to scrimmage. All this was so exciting. I loved it. I could hardly wait until Saturday – I could do basketball; I was good at it.

Being able to help. I became a safety kid helping students cross the street, and I loved this. I was doing something that I was good at, helping others – and that felt great. One day the principal came to me in class and pulled me out, gave me a machete, and sent me out to the playground and asked me to cut some small trees that were growing all over the playground. Evidently, a student had fallen on one of the sharp-ended trees and got hurt. So, there I was working at something I could do; it was a good feeling. I have remembered that experience to this day.

In grade school, the school building was set up on a hill, a large hill, and it was hard walking up to the school from my house. Then there was the long climb down; this I did every day. There were no buses for me. I think it was in the fifth or sixth grade when I got a bicycle for Christmas or a birthday.

My bicycle. Oh, how exciting and wonderful to have a bike and ride it around the neighborhood! We lived in a neighborhood that wasn't too busy with cars. You could ride for four or maybe six blocks and be safe, and so my parents let me do this until I got better at riding. However, I can remember a time when dad was driving a car. I was riding my bike and I turned to cross the street, and dad was there in the car, watching me. It was awful. He naturally scolded me thoroughly about being safe. That set me back for a while. I soon got to ride my bike to school, but that hill was hard to climb with a bike. Going home was wonderful, going down that hill. Oh, it was fast. What excitement and joy I had then!

During this time, I got a paper route. I was the paper boy in the neighborhood. I could ride my bike and pass out papers. This also started my business adventures; earning money was great.

I remember asking my parents if I could garden in the backyard. They said yes. Oh my - my own garden! It was a little plot. I had only a shovel to make a hole, and that was my rototiller. That was hard work for a little kid, but I loved it. I remember planting tomatoes, onions, lettuce, and green beans. The tomatoes were the best. There's something about hot summers and Ohio weather that makes tomatoes absolutely great. What a taste! They would melt in your mouth with a little salt. My love affair with gardening had begun.

Here was something I could do and get praised for it; what could be better to please dad and mom?

Our dogs. Dad always had a dog. They were always Fox Terriers - scrappy, barking dogs. I'm sure mother just put up with them. She seemed to like animals, but dad only liked dogs. I used to go to the playground with my dog, and lay down in the summer, with the sun beating down on my body, relaxing me. My dog would lay by my side, or I would put my head on his belly. Together we enjoyed the hot summer days being lazy. I still love dogs.

I spent many an hour playing basketball with the neighborhood kids. I would practice and practice. I thought I became a pretty good basketball player. I continued playing until I was 38 years old. I became a basketball coach for high school kids. I taught my son Tim how to play basketball. I played basketball during the two years I went to college. I also coached and played in a Church of God basketball league for many years.

There was a manhole cover where I could go down into the sewer that collected rain run-off. This pipe ran for miles. It also ran under the canal and came up to the strip of land between the canal and the river. It was scary. I carried a flashlight and did this a few times, going in different directions. I decided this probably wasn't the safest thing to do, and I stopped it.

Building a boat. I played with a boy named Larry, who lived about half a block away from me. His house was right up against the huge flood levee. On the other side was a canal that fed water to a paper mill. This levee ran for miles. The Great Miami River fed this canal. The levee was for flood control. This was also my playground. There was a bridge that crossed this canal to a large strip of land between the canal and the river. Here are some things we did, and of course, my dog was always with me - playing on the levee, going across the bridge to the strip of land that ran for miles.

One day I got a great idea to build a boat in Larry's back-yard. We took machetes and climbed trees to cut large vines to make a skeleton boat. Then I went to a hardware store and talked the owner into giving me an account so I could buy canvas to put around the vines which would make the boat float. Of course, dad didn't know anything about this. I was in seventh heaven for a while. Larry and I tried to cover the skeleton boat with canvas. Then there was the problem of how to carry such a heavy boat up the huge canal levee. By then, my dad had found out about the canvas, and took the canvas back to the store. Dad didn't pay for it, and I was in trouble. However, I didn't get spanked.

One day I was playing on the strip of land between the canal and the river and decided to build a fire, so I did. It was a small fire for a while. I didn't pay too close attention, and the fire grew larger, and larger. Oh my, I was in trouble. How-ever, I took something that was a big cloth, my coat or a sleeping bag, and beat the fire out. Nobody knew this be-cause I was alone.

I played around with trapping small rodents that were in the canal, such as muskrats, opossums, and one time, I caught a duck. I started feeling sorry for these animals, and I stopped trapping them.

Trees. I loved to climb trees. I would climb very tall trees. One time I climbed a tall, tall tree that was higher than houses. I could look down on the rooftops. Boy, I was really up there. Then, all of a sudden, I slipped. I was falling and falling. I stuck out my arms and legs to catch myself on other branches. I finally stopped my falling. My arms and sides got bruised up, and I was hurt, but I recovered.

The parents of my friend Larry wanted a large tree limb taken down from a tree hanging over their garage. I thought I could do this without any trouble. Larry and I got a saw and started cutting, and about halfway through, I thought it might fall and put a hole in the roof of the garage, so I tied a rope onto the limb. I cut and cut; it was hard work. The limb was not coming free of the tree. Then I made a big mistake: I climbed between the roof and the tree limb, and the branch broke free, hitting me, knocking me totally unconscious. I fell off the garage roof. The next thing I knew I was on the ground. I woke up, wondering what happened. Larry and his parents were thankful that I was okay - a big relief for them, and I thought I was invincible. I thought, what's the matter with you guys, I'm all right.

Larry and I fell out of friendship over something - I don't remember what it was. I think maybe it was because my dad had a paint and wallpaper store and a restaurant, and perhaps they were jealous of this. We never made up. I always felt guilty about holding resentment towards him about something. I didn't forgive him even though he asked me to. I just couldn't do it. My parents and his parents also were involved. Now I wish that I had forgiven him, but life moves on, and no one is perfect.

They needed someone to clean the windows of the shops where my Dad's store was, so dad got me to do this. Other retail stores in downtown Franklin needed their windows to be cleaned as well, so on Saturdays I would work cleaning retail store windows and made some money. You see, work was the most important thing in life, and of course, I enjoyed making money. Now I had a paper route and a window washing business. During my high school years, dad bought property on the edge of town, and I asked him if I could plant a large, very large garden. He said yes. There was a problem that showed up later: there wasn't water to the property, you had to depend on the weather. Ohio is very hot during the summer - however, I didn't think about that. I went full bore and planted 1,000 tomato plants and lots of corn. It wasn't a complete disaster. I did get some corn, and some tomatoes. Again, I went door to door selling tomatoes and corn. Of course, it gave my family some good eating.

A budding entrepreneur. We had some friends who were farmers. They had lots of chickens and had eggs to sell. I started an egg route, delivering eggs to my neighbors. I would buy them from the farmer and sell them for a profit. When I buy eggs in grocery stores now, I am amazed that they don't cost very much. In the back yard we had a cherry tree, and mom would can cherries every year and make cherry pies. These trees were for pie cherries. My brothers and I would pick the cherries and go door to door selling the cherries in order to make money.

High school. My high school years began in seventh grade, as my classes were in the high school. So we got to fellowship with the upper classmen and, of course, we would go to different rooms for individual subjects. When the bell rang, we would change classrooms. This was different, as in the lower grades you stayed in one room. It seemed scary to me, moving up, but I handled it okay. Again, I struggled with reading and writing, and again, the school bullies would pick on me and I would have fights on the school grounds. This got me into trouble; my guardian angel, the former principal, was no longer looking out for me. I had new teachers, and principals, and it seemed to me that they read my transcripts of failing grades, and I could do nothing to change those grades. It seemed to me the teachers were against me, and I started becoming a little paranoid, feeling that it was hopeless trying to get good grades. Of course, this was not true.

I would take the easiest classes. Industrial arts was a great class for me, and cooking class was great. I loved history class, even though I had to listen to mom read the material. Oh yes: I had a history teacher who was in the Battle of the Bulge during WWII. I tried to get him to tell me about the war. He said it was very, very, very cold. He didn't talk much about it. I did love history, as I was extremely curious about WWII.

The other class I enjoyed was health class, and I remember being very curious about the digestive tract, the stomach, and the intestines. To me, that was amazing. I don't remember anything about being taught about being a sexual being, and I certainly wish someone would have mentioned that. I was extremely curious about what a woman looked like, how babies were born, where they came from. I think this was normal, but mom and dad didn't talk about it. So, I had to pick it up from my peers, which didn't really help much.

My football career started in grade school and continued through high school. This was somewhat expected by the family. My dad played football, and my uncles played football. My uncles would tell me stories of their glory days playing the game. My dad was pretty silent about his days. He did show us that he earned a letter for being an outstanding football player. He had it sewn to a sweater. It was the letter F for Franklin High School.

Playing halfback. As halfback, I scored lots of touchdowns. I was good at dodging the other players trying to tackle me. What did I learn from playing football? Well, in high school we had to cope with losing seasons. We did win some games. There was a big shakeup in the high school one year because players were getting drunk, and I got moved up from eighth grade football to high school, because those players got kicked off of the team. Naturally, with eighth graders playing against junior and senior high school players, we got beat. We would practice before school started in the Fall, but the weather was terribly hot. We worked out in the hot sun. Oh my, how terrible it was to sweat. We took salt tablets to try to hold water in our bodies. Also, if you didn't do what the coach said, or if we lost a game, we had to run up a steep hill for punishment. Oh my, it was painful. I was a pretty good player. I also loved to play linebacker, and tackle those offensive players running the ball. I also played defensive halfback. I loved to intercept those long passes, and also catch the kickoffs and try to run for a touchdown. Sometimes I would do those things, and I would get some praise.

There was a lot of pain and difficulty during those years. I was expected to play, and yes, there were great experiences and joy in playing, but there was the challenge of getting in shape. I learned to stick to it, to work through it, to stay the course. Also, I learned teamwork, working together for a purpose. I had good times and bad times playing football. In my teens I was injured with a hernia, and had surgery to repair that.

I was also punished by the school system. They would not let me play my senior year because of my age and my poor marks in reading and writing. This hurt, but what could I do?

When I was a freshman in Butler, PA, the school wouldn't let me play basketball. However, they made a mistake in football, they didn't report my age to the league, so in my sophomore year, I got to play football. I think they didn't turn it in to the league, because they would have had to forfeit all the games because I was too old. But good for me; I got to play on the sophomore team. From my point of view, they were wrong with their rules, the punishment for bad grades and my being set back two years.

Moving to Butler, Pennsylvania, dad and mom rented out our house in Franklin and we stayed with my Uncle Eston Doty until dad and mom found a home in Butler. Staying with the Dotys for a short while was a real adventure, a great time. They attended the Presbyterian Church, and I went to church with them. But I felt so out of place, because the Sunday school class had well educated teenagers who could read and write well. The people going to that church were highly educated, and I didn't want to go back, I felt so outclassed.

The house in Butler was huge, with beautiful interior wood, stained dark. There was a stairway going upstairs to the bathroom and bedrooms. Downstairs there was a huge kitchen, dining room, living room, and, of course, a basement. There was a garage. This was on a hillside. This was my sophomore year of high school, and I started to date more, falling in love with a girl named Marilyn – oh, she was beautiful. She was Catholic, but I didn't believe that was a problem. I think if we had stayed in Butler, I would have tried to marry her.

I wasn't driving a car yet, so when I dated, I would arrange transportation to movies, dances and going skating. I was also very embarrassed, not being able to read or pronounce words, names, or places very well. This would show up at times. I also couldn't read or remember names or places. I had to work out my own system. It seemed to me that I did well at this. My ability to talk and to communicate grew, and I learned to handle things.

Something happened with dad's job at the MacGraw Construction Company. I don't think Mom wanted to leave Butler. I'm not sure what was going on at that time. Dad didn't talk; silence was his way. So shortly after that we moved back to Franklin. Dad went back to private survey work.

I was a junior in high school at this point. I played football but didn't make the basketball team. That was a big disappointment; however, I played basketball in the local parks every time I could.

Denny was in Korea at this time. When you look at his pictures, you could tell he was trim and in great physical shape, the best of his life. He told us the North Koreans would come across the DMZ and try to kill them. They had fire fights. I know this had to have greatly affected Denny mentally.

Before Denny left for the service, he gave me many driving lessons. I learned to drive in a secret way, without my parents knowing. I studied and studied and studied the driver's manual. Then, with Denny gone to the military, I asked mom if she would help me with my driver's test. Dad was against it. He refused to let me go and take the test, but mother took me. I passed with flying colors. Dad couldn't believe that I passed the test. Oh, what a great victory for me, a step forward! It was freedom from my dad, I was becoming an adult. What a great feeling of accomplishment.

A bad illness. During my junior year, I caught the Asian flu, and was very sick. This was during football season, and I missed three games. Football was very important for me. After I recovered from my sickness, I got out of bed and played in the football game that Friday, but I was not in good physical shape because I had been in bed for the past three weeks. I took up my positions as running halfback and defensive halfback that particular game. I played my heart out and became physically exhausted. We were losing, and in the last minute or two of the game, I intercepted a pass and tried to run for a touchdown, but I was spent and exhausted. I did the best I could, running as fast as I could, but it must've seemed in slow motion to those who were watching.

After the game, a great friend came to me and asked what was wrong, and I told him I was exhausted. What hurt the most was that later, the coach asked me if I had been smoking too many cigarettes and thus couldn't run any faster. Of course, people watching from the stands didn't know I had spent the last three weeks in bed with the flu. Again, there was someone in a position of authority over me. This was very, very hurtful to me. After the game, my parents sent me to the family doctor because I was in bad shape, and very exhausted, probably dehydrated again. I disappointed those around me. I recovered, and in practice the next week, the coaches had me work out longer and harder to get me back in shape, so that next week I would play better.

One of the things that became a part of my life was the feeling that everyone was superior to me, and that I needed their help. I would pursue their ideas and advice as being the greatest. In some ways, I was codependent on others, and not becoming my own person, or thinking for myself. I thought my grandmother on my mother's side was the greatest. She also believed in God. She was a Methodist, and I picked up on this thinking. Man, if God would just help me, I would get the guidance that I needed. I prayed all the time, especially at night when I went to bed. I would pray, it seemed, for hours, thinking over everything that happened that day. This, of course, became the foundation for my OCD, obsessive-compulsive disorder, thinking and thinking and thinking everything over and over, and planning and planning for doing things better next time.

In my senior year of high school, I was punished by the school system, and not allowed to play any sports. In a way, we all lost. They lost because they did not fulfill their goal of helping students. I lost because of the rejection and the embarrassment I felt from my peers.

One thing I did like about myself was that I felt I was good-looking. I also had good common sense. I had worked out a system of getting along with my peers, and with those who had authority over me. I was a peacemaker at home, between my parents. I tried hard to grow in every way possible.

CHAPTER FOUR: A YOUNG ADULT, GIRLS AND RELIGION

Fundamentalist Christian denominations include those within several Pentecostal, Charismatic, Evangelical, and conservative non-denominational movements. Though certain beliefs vary from group to group, Fundamentalist denominations tend to have these attributes in common: They believe in the literal truth and inerrancy of the Bible, along with the literal virgin birth of Christ; they emphasize original sin and human depravity, and the need to accept Christ as one's Savior in order to avoid eternal damnation; they believe in a literal Heaven and Hell, along with actual angels, demons, and Satan; and they seek to filter out diverse beliefs and worldviews that conflict with their own.

Those who leave such denominations may experience symptoms of RTS (Religious Trauma Syndrome), which include, but are not limited to, learned helplessness, identity confusion, dissociation, sleep and eating disorders, substance abuse, anxiety, depression, and interpersonal dysfunction. Critical thinking and independent thought are often underdeveloped. Since the term is still so new, and quantitative research is needed, there are no clear estimates as to how many

*people who leave their faith end up developing RTS. Also, Psycholo-
gist Dr. Marlene Winell ("Leaving the Fold") notes that aspects of
RTS can develop in those who have not yet left their faith, especially
those symptoms related to helplessness, problems regarding authority, and many others, making RTS estimates even more difficult to
calculate. Interestingly, Dr. Winell has anecdotally noticed that certain personality traits seem related to the development of RTS, including high levels of devotion and commitment and an analytical
nature.*

- *From "The Hidden Trauma of Life After Fundamentalism" by
  Kristen Hovet*

It was my senior year in high school, and like every normal high school student, I was trying my best to accept
all these changes that were coming. Puberty was upon
me, graduating from high school was upon me, and leaving
my parents' nest was upon me. Oh my, how was this going
to work out?

Looking for a good wife. When I was around 15 years old,
I started praying that God would help me find a good wife.
This was a prayer that I asked over and over again. I had dated
a number of girls, and I was starting to become aware of my
sexual attraction to them. This was normal, but I was also
trying to deny this attraction. There was locker room brag-
ging among boys, and a few girls getting pregnant in my senior year. I also noticed a twenty-something female teacher
making out in a car with a high school star athlete, of football

and basketball fame. I was so upset about this. I started praying that God would help me find a pure girl that I could date. To my surprise, a new girl showed up in my classes. She was a preacher's daughter of the Church of God. Of course, I asked her for a date, and we became a couple. She invited me to attend church services, which I did. Was this to be the girl of my dreams and prayers? Naturally, I thought this was a strong possibility. In some ways, this was a very happy time for me, but it was also a nightmare because of the church teachings and doctrine.

I turned to the church for counseling about the girl. I felt the pastor was absolutely no help, but what could he do? I was lovesick. The church had a lot of rules: you can't do things such as dancing, mixed gender swimming, picture shows. There were other things that Christians, according to them, didn't do. I became very confused about these things. Their basic doctrine was, you needed to confess your sins, and then you received salvation. You then became baptized by dipping in a baptismal tub, completely under water. You then still needed to receive the Holy Spirit, called the second work of grace. When you received the second work of grace you would not sin again because God is helping you with His holy guidance. This was a holiness group that demanded perfection, and a long list of dos and don'ts. Today I consider this a cult, where they systematically start to control your mind and thinking.

I kept going to this church, and seeking God's help, thinking that perhaps this was God guiding me, in finding the girl of my prayers and dreams. The first time I went to the altar to beg for forgiveness for my sins, the pastor's wife told me I couldn't get saved until I gave up dancing and accepted their rules. I went away totally confused, but finally they accepted me as being saved and I went forward with baptism. I went to the altar for forgiveness many, many, many more times, to the point that they asked me not to go any more.

Totally consumed. The leaders of the church asked me to preach on Wednesdays, and they asked me to become a youth counselor. Oh wow - somebody was saying to me that I was a worthwhile person! And I loved being a leader. This was so magnificent for me. Yet I didn't realize that I would be pulling away from my family, and my friends, and would be totally consumed by church. My time from there on was church, church, and church.

Was I being called to be a preacher? Could God help me overcome my confusion and handicap? Of course, I thought that I could rise to the challenge that was before me. My life seemed to be almost more than I could handle. Guilt, and more guilt, was put upon me by the preaching of the church in Franklin, Ohio, demanding that I be perfect.

My Obsessive-Compulsive Disorder and depression were now upon me. I learned to handle it by going forth in silence. However, my mind was processing these new ideas. All the time, in some ways, I was miserable, but I couldn't leave these people who said I was a person of great importance. Their teaching I really didn't accept. I just didn't understand what they were saying, but I thought I would understand their teachings in the future, and peace would become mine.

Strict church doctrines. Some churches affiliated with the Church of God believed that roller skating, swimming, dancing, picture shows, make-up, jewelry, ties, short dresses, bikinis, television, were all sins. Their doctrine, on the second work of grace, was that salvation cut down the tree of sin, and sanctification was rooting out the root system of the tree, and one had to be perfect in all things, or you needed to start all over again. This was terrible for me. Also, I depended upon the local pastor and his beliefs, his training, his education.

Of course, at this time in my life, I didn't know that each church taught a different doctrine, but the basic belief of many of these churches held that you must be perfect, or God will reject you. You must go through the basic two steps of salvation: asking for forgiveness, and sanctification. Some churches taught a third step of total re-dedication, which was three trips to the altar to get rid of your guilt.

This, of course, was, in some ways, how I was raised. Dad used fear and guilt to control us kids. It was hard for me to place a balance in my life because of what the churches were saying: total all or nothing commitment to perfection. And I knew that the truth was, I couldn't be perfect. Therefore, I always felt guilty in evangelistic services of the church.

Preachers who preached that way, many of them, counted success by how many worshipers they could get to go to the altar, which meant they preached to make people feel guilty.

However, I was very interested in the preacher's daughter, and was getting a great deal of acceptance and praise from the Franklin Church of God, so I couldn't leave this church. I was caught between a rock and hard place. What I needed to hear was that God accepted me and loved me just the way I was. But instead, I heard hell and damnation, and in order to have God's blessings, I needed to work and be perfect. Later in my life, I understood that God did accept me, and loves me just the way I am, but it took many years for that to happen.

PART TWO: BECOMING AN ADULT

••

CHAPTER ONE: COLLEGE, AND FINDING A CHURCH THAT WORKED

··

Portland is the largest and most populous city in the state of Oregon and the seat of Multnomah County. It is a major port in the Willamette Valley region of the Pacific Northwest, at the confluence of the Willamette and Columbia rivers in Northwestern Oregon. As of 2019, Portland had an estimated population of 654,741, making it the 26th most populated city in the United States, the sixth-most populous on the West Coast, and the second-most populous in the Pacific Northwest after Seattle. Approximately 2.4 million people live in the Portland metropolitan statistical area (MSA), making it the 25th most populous in the United States. Approximately 47% of Oregon's population resides within the Portland metropolitan area.

Named after Portland, Maine, the Oregon settlement began to be populated in the 1830s near the end of the Oregon Trail. Its water access provided convenient transportation of goods, and the timber industry was a major force in the city's early economy. Beginning in the 1960s, Portland became noted for its growing progressive political values, earning it a reputation as a bastion of counterculture. Among its institutions of higher education are Portland State University, Reed College, and Warner Pacific College.

Portland was the first city to enact a comprehensive plan to re-duce carbon dioxide emissions. In 2018, a national survey ranked Portland as the 10th greenest city in the nation. Its climate is marked by warm, dry summers and cool, rainy winters. This climate is ideal for growing roses, and Portland has been called the "City of Roses" for over a century.

- *Wikipedia*

Because I was doing so well at being a youth counselor and preaching, I did have good skills communicating through talking. I could read on, probably, a third-grade level. It seemed to me that I was being called to the ministry, and that my struggle with guilt would surely go away. I started thinking about going to college, and I announced to the world I was called to be a minister, and, of course, my family looked on with amazement. In Anderson, Indiana there was a Church of God college, which looked to me to be expensive. At that time, a kind family moved to Franklin and started attending the Franklin Church of God. Their son, Bob, was 18 years old and wanted to go to Warner Pacific College in Oregon, another Church of God college. I had heard of the college, and knew that it was cheaper. I had two weeks to decide if I wanted to go with Bob. I had a 1956 Chevy, and Bob needed transportation to Portland, Oregon. I decided to come to Warner to pursue becoming a minister. In many ways this was wonderful, and in many ways this was terrible. It was a mixed bag at best. I had not resolved my guilt with evangelism. This would be a problem for me for many years to come.

Before I left for Oregon, my Guardian Angel, Mr. Faley, the school principal who helped me in grade school, came to see me, and was very concerned about me getting caught up with the Church of God. He knew my parents were Presbyterian. He warned my parents about this situation. However, my parents and I disregarded his concern. I never heard from him again. He was a true friend to my parents and watched out for me and Denny and Mike.

Off to the Northwest. Of course, it was exciting and a great adventure to see some of the United States of America. One of the big benefits was that I was going to be 3,000 miles away from a controlling dad, and I could start learning how to be on my own. I would start learning how to make my own decisions, and become my own person, learn how to stand on my own two feet. My friend and I enjoyed driving through the different states to get to Oregon; we visited Yellowstone National Park, and Mt. Rushmore. These places we enjoyed; however, when we got to Oregon, and drove next to the Columbia River and Gorge, and went up to Crown Point, I kid you not, my mouth dropped open. I was overwhelmed with the beauty of Multnomah Falls. Oh my, such glory. I fell in love with Oregon.

There was lots of excitement driving up for the first time to see the college campus, and finding out where we were going to live, and getting lined up for our classes and seeing where those were going to be. At that time, Warner Pacific didn't have a gymnasium. However, I learned that they played basketball in the local high schools. Bob and I started out rooming together in the college dorm. It was very noisy with lots of other students around, but I was going to make the best of it.

Once enrolled in college, I took Bible studies, both New Testament and Old Testament. I also had to take English classes and history classes. What a challenge I had before me, trying to read and stay up with all the assignments. I joined the ministerial student society, and to my amazement they asked me to be vice president of this group. I made new friends and met the professors. I wanted to be accepted and make a contribution to everybody. Of course, I flunked my English class. To my amazement I did pull a C as a semester grade, so I passed all my classes except English. I did extremely well at playing sports. I met the man who coached the basketball team. I joined the team and played guard. I played better than the other guards. However, because of not passing English classes, I was not allowed to play first string. The player who was playing first string came to me and apologized, saying he knew that I should be playing first string. Oh well, I took it in stride. From my point of view, I had been there and done that. I learned in high school that nothing in life is fair all the time.

The huge, huge spider. Here's a little story from my two years at Warner Pacific College. There was a half basement underneath the dorm where we were staying. There was a laundry room down there, and there was a science biology classroom, as well. I would use the washer and dryer next to the science room. When I was doing this, nobody else was around. Suddenly one night, I saw a huge, huge spider crawling around in the laundry room. I became very scared. I thought maybe it came from South America, where food was sent up with fruit or bananas and this spider had hitched a ride in one of the crates. I found a wet mop, and I beat that spider to death, thinking I had saved some peoples' lives. Later, I learned this spider was part of the science class instruction and had escaped from its cage. The professors were disappointed that I killed their specimen, but of course I didn't know. I was about saving my life and other people's lives.

Looking for a good church. I started out going to Woodstock Church of God, and other students piled in my 1956 Chevrolet and came along. It was fun to be with a group! However, my enjoyment didn't last long. The pastors were very evangelistic, hell and brimstone ministers. This caused me great pain. I saw myself as missing the mark. I couldn't be perfect, so guilt was heaped upon me by this type of preaching. And again, I held my head high, and didn't talk to preachers about this. To my amazement, they asked me if I would be their youth counselor. Of course, I couldn't say no, and of course I told everybody that I was going to be a minister. Somehow, some way, I was going to get there. Also, to my amazement, my reading skills started to improve and improve during the two years I attended college. From the outside, it looked like I was well on my way, and it appeared to me that people saw that I was a leader. Why else would they ask me to take leadership roles? But inside, I was confused about the church and its doctrine. Funny thing about the West Coast: It was very liberal. Some churches thought picture shows were okay, TV was okay, and some even accepted dancing. This also brought about a lot of unanswered questions for me about who was a Christian: if some did these things, and some didn't do these things, who was right?

After the first year of college, some of my professors suggested that I start psychological counseling with Wade, a counselor who was also a preacher at Holladay Park Church of God. This was a great thing, to start counseling. Wade helped me see that I was not called to be a minister. We started working on what I understood was my depression, changing my views of accepting myself with the skills and talents that I had, and learning to accept my sexuality. This wasn't going to happen overnight. It's difficult to change when you spend twenty years learning to think a certain way. You see, I couldn't accept myself because my goal was to improve and grow into being perfect because my father demanded that I know everything about everything and be perfect in everything. This is how I interpreted things. Of course, the counselor didn't know about my processing disorder. I really believe my mind was working on rewiring itself, so as I grew older my ability to compensate was getting better.

The wrong girl, right outcome. During this time, I got engaged to a college student. Oh boy, this was the wrong girl at the wrong time, and in the wrong place. She was looking for a minister to marry, and I seemed to fill this goal of hers. When she learned that I had trouble reading and pronouncing words and understanding what people said to me, I no longer met her goals, and she broke up with me. At the time, I was broken hearted, but it was the best thing that could have happened.

While I was in counseling with Wade, he advised me to change churches. By this time, I was in my second year of college, and because of a room shortage, I was living upstairs in the parsonage of the Richmond Church of God. The pastor was very kind, patient, generous, and a gentle preacher who knew what he was doing. It was natural that I attend Richmond Church of God. I had found a place of comfort, good guidance, good preaching, and could bring healing and peace to my soul. But I had a very, very long journey to bring mental health to my life. I resigned being vice president of the student body Ministerial Association, and I resigned being youth pastor of Woodstock Church of God. However, before I quit those things, I went to care centers and preached, or gave a little talk, many times on the weekends. I also traveled to Idaho and preached in different churches. I also preached at Woodstock on occasions. I always have been gutsy, a big risk taker. Sometimes I would win, sometimes I would lose.

I did love teaching and talking to people about life and a belief in God. I really felt that God's hand was upon me. However, I realized that I had misunderstood His calling, and would question future callings of my own, and question when other people said they were called to do something for God. Perhaps this was the way God was to put distance between dad and me, starting my long journey to deal with the cards that had been dealt me. You don't choose your parents, and you don't necessarily inherit the best genes. I feel sorry for people born with schizophrenic mental disorder; they don't have a choice.

Just think of the great company I keep with others who have struggled with depression, such as Winston Churchill, Abraham Lincoln, Adlai Stevenson, Mike Wallace, Terry Bradshaw; these are only a few. I think they say one in three people struggle with depression. This is a chemical imbalance in your brain, and you can't do much about it. You have to live with it and do the best you can. It is a treatable illness with proper medication. My problem was that all the different kinds of medications that I tried didn't always help. They often made things worse for me; but others have found medications that have helped them.

Religion and my pursuit of God: I didn't realize that my prayers would someday be answered in very peculiar ways.

Yes, I needed help. Yes, I now needed to take responsibility for myself, and others, regardless of the poor foundation that my parents and the school system gave me. I had to forgive them, which God asked me to do, and which I did.

CHAPTER TWO: GAIL, GAIL, GAIL

····························

Gail and I have been married for almost sixty years. Gail asked if she could write down some of her thoughts to be included in my life story. Gail has been a huge part of my entire life story and what she decided to share has touched me deeply. She is the love of my life for so many reasons. Here is her letter:

My name is Gail Hanson Burroughs.

Who am I? I am the daughter of Howard and Erma Hanson. My father was mentally ill with OCD (Obsessive-Compulsive Disorder). He was obsessed with religion. His purpose in life was to tell everyone that they were evil and full of the carnal nature. My mother's purpose was to love my father, and she supported him. When harsh words came from her husband, she ignored them and pretended they weren't there. They were like the wind that comes and goes and means nothing.

When we were dating, my husband-to-be Chuck called me his 1930s girl. He was my knight in shining armor. He became my man, my lover, and the person I have supported with unconditional love. That is what my mother taught me. I wanted to shout it from the rooftops; I found my man! I am so proud to be Chuck's wife. I support him and love him unconditionally. I ignore harsh words from my husband. I believe in him.

I wanted babies. I was a stay-at-home mom. My job was to raise our children and take care of the house and support my husband.

Before we were married, Chuck told me he couldn't read or write very well. He told me he has learning disabilities. This absolutely did not matter to me. I told him we will get through this together. A college degree did not matter to me. My job was to support and help Chuck. I did get what I wanted – a husband. He is beyond complicated – indeed, a very complicated man. He has his demons, but he, without question, has worked at changing himself to be a good husband and a loving father to our children. Chuck loves me in a physical way more than I could ever imagine. He is a great lover.

Chuck has an amazing work ethic. He is very successful at making decisions for our whole family. We are successful financially. Our marriage has lasted almost 60 years. Our children are all raised, and all are doing well.

I love the people of the church, all of my friends. I love to sing and have sung in choirs and ladies' groups for years. I loved to stay at home and take care of our house. That is what I wanted. My dreams have been fulfilled. My husband loves me unconditionally, and I love him unconditionally. He says that we make music together, and that we do. I loved being a contractor's wife, being with Chuck. We have been together 24 hours a day, seven days a week.

We are best friends.

- Gail Hanson Burroughs

Falling in love. Oh my, every time I was near Gail I felt this strong, very strong attraction to her like a magnet to steel. However, it seemed to me like there were ten guys ahead of me. She was dating others and her work schedule was different than mine. The hours, so it seemed to me, made it impossible to get a date with her. During the summer of 1960, I was working for Warner Pacific College in maintenance and repair and cutting the grass. I was off work getting an ice cream treat at the Dairy Queen when Gail and others came in and asked me to go to the beach with them. I was engaged at that time to another girl. Still, I said yes, I would go. Gail and I rode in the back seat together. Oh, what an attraction. We had a ball running and playing on the beach together. What a time we had. This was going to be the start for Gail and me. We were going to be together on other dates and outings in the future, but I didn't know this for sure yet. And of course, some of the college students talked to my fiancée about Gail and me going to the beach. When we started back to college that fall, my fiancée broke up with me. Praise the Lord. Of course, I didn't realize what a blessing this would be for my future.

I don't know when Gail heard about my breaking up with my fiancée, but all of a sudden Gail was in my life. Those other boys were gone, and I was number one. I think she was pursuing me, and I was consumed with becoming a minister. Giving up this pursuit was hard because I was so convinced that God wanted me to become a preacher. One evening Gail and I and another college couple, Don and Nina, went to the chapel to pray. Little did I know that this would be an extremely significant time in my life that I would never forget. As I prayed, it seemed to me that God spoke to me and said, I love you, I love you, wait upon me and I will give you direction. After praying, we were walking around campus, and I told Gail, Don and Nina that I felt that God spoke these words to me. In my mind, at least: you can imagine all the anxiety and confusion that was going on with my life. At this time, I was in a lot of emotional pain. I was still counseling with a minister. I needed to change directions. I needed to see things differently and pursue a different course for my life. I had changed churches by then and was getting along much better in church. I had a good relationship with everybody. I had made lots of new friends, and before dating Gail, I had dated quite a number of girls on campus and off-campus, high school seniors whom I met. However, by this time, Gail was number one. I was playing basketball at this time, too, which was great for me. There was something I needed to tell Gail. I had big problems, and it seemed to me they were going to take years to work out. I didn't think that having depression and obsessive-compulsive disorder meant that I was mentally ill. None of this made sense to me. But I needed to tell her in an honest way that I needed time to work these things out to discover what was going on with me. I was trying to make sense out of my life at this time.

Gail went to her dorm room after I told her that we should wait at least two years. I was talking about marriage without saying it. Later, I learned that she got depressed over this, not really understanding. On dates, we hiked the trails of the Columbia Gorge, including Horsetail Falls trail. The church, at that time, owned some property and a cabin out in the Gorge, near Multnomah Falls. One time we went there for a date.

A very special radio. I was working as a custodian cleaning up grade schools at night to help pay the bills. I told Gail that I didn't have a radio and it would be nice if I could listen to music while I worked. I didn't think too much about this, but one night I got off work, and it was dark. I had my car and drove to the Parsonage. I got out of my car and started walking to the back door and out of the shadows stepped Gail. She had a small radio for me. Wow, double wow. She got my attention. She liked me, perhaps even loved me, I didn't know for sure. But this was a very, very good sign.

Rev. Arthur Ely was pastor of the Richmond Church of God. I remember cooking a meal for Gail at the Ely's house. They left their house so we could be alone. One time Gail got sick with the flu while living in the girl's dorm. I cooked some chicken noodle soup and took it up to the girl's dorm. I had to throw rocks up to her window to get her attention. She lived on the third floor, but I got her attention. She came down to get the soup.

Perhaps because I was so attracted to her, we double dated and made sure someone was with us. This way, I showed deep respect for her. I felt we should base our relationship on who we were, to see if we would be compatible with one another. So, it wasn't based on sex. But, of course, we were attracted to each other. As I remember, we were sitting on a grassy hillside on campus of WPC and I said to her, "Should we get married this year or next year?" She said we could get married that year. I was concerned about money. We drove up to Mount Tabor Park and made out a budget; that was how I thought. Gail could care less about money and budgets. She wanted to get married.

Wow! I thought then, and still do, that marriage is about helping one another grow together.

I remember my counselor, Wade, looking at Gail with sad eyes and facial expressions, thinking Gail was probably going to be in trouble with me as her husband. That look hurt deep down inside of me. However, now that Gail and I have been married for well over 50 years, I can say that I gave her a wonderful life, and she would say that was true.

How did God guide me as I waited for him to do so? I dropped out of college, married Gail, and went to work for Blue Bus lines. Their main parking lot and garages were in Tigard. I went to work for them as a grease monkey. I washed and cleaned the buses at night. I drove the school bus early in the morning and evening. I also went out and picked up broken-down buses and brought them back to the yard.

The wedding. We were poor college kids. We had college bills to pay off. Gail and I had $100 between us. Gail made her own wedding dress. A couple related to our pastor made our wedding cake for us very, very cheaply. Pastor Ely's wife helped Gail pick out the flowers. Gail asked me to go out to the little house that the Elys were going to rent to us. Gail wanted us to make the bed that we were going to sleep in for the first time after we were married. Oh my! I helped her make it, but for me, it was not a comfortable thing to do. It put a lot of pressure on me. I hadn't really accepted my sexuality as a human being. I was upset, and of course, Gail picked up these vibes. And I later asked Mrs. Ely to comfort Gail; she said this would be hard for a man to do.

Rev. Ely married us. I remember the Reverend looking at me so sternly as I said our vows. I wondered, would I be a good husband, or painful to Gail? That look would stay with me the rest of my life. My best man was Bob Tyler. Don Wood and Ken Smatlack also stood up with me. The church people went all out to help us. Sister Ely helped Gail in many ways, with her wedding dress, and giving other advice. The Elys had a one-bedroom house on an acre of land at SE 167th and Stephens St. in Portland, Oregon that we rented for five years. Gail would have to tell you the names of other people who helped with our wedding. Gail's folks, Erma and Howard Hanson, drove out for the wedding from Cedar Rapids, Iowa. My folks decided not to come, but agreed to help us come to Ohio later. Ken Hanson, Gail's brother, attended the wedding, and also sang at the service. Some college friends decorated our car and put tin cans on the back. I thought that people would chase us in other cars. One thing I do remember was someone shouting, "watch Oregon grow." Of course, they were right.

My best man, Bob, had become a good friend. He, like me, was searching for which way to go in life. He had already become a barber, and I bet that probably became his occupation later in life, I don't know. I lost track of him after leaving college.

A world's fair honeymoon. Bob arranged for us to go to the world's fair in Seattle and stay in somebody's house who was vacationing elsewhere. We stayed there for free. What a deal! But the first night was at our little rental house in Portland. Oh boy, oh boy - what a time that was for Gail and me! Our first night was an experience of great joy for me. It was a night to remember. We were both virgins with no guilt about experiences of past adventures. Even after we met, I had no idea that she was to become the wife that I had prayed for, as we were so, so different. But we were to grow in our love for one another, and we learned how to negotiate our differences. I believed that I would become a great lover as we explored the joys of sexual pleasure that all young couples experience. Our son Tim was conceived on our honeymoon. The World's Fair was a secondary concern, something we did after the exhaustion of our honeymoon. We had very little money, so we couldn't do much at the World's Fair anyway.

We attended the Sunday morning church service in Seattle. We looked at the Space Needle, wishing we could afford to eat in the restaurant on top. I don't remember how many days we spent in Seattle, probably three days, but soon it was back to Portland and work. However, later on, on one of our anniversaries, we spent time in Seattle and ate in the restaurant on top of the Space Needle. Oh boy; by that time, I was on the way to financial security, and could afford to splurge.

CHAPTER THREE: MAKING A LIVING

....

The painting business. Back to Portland after the honeymoon. Sometime around this time, I started working for a friend I met through the Church of God. He was married, and going to college to become a minister, except as I got to know him, I came to believe that he was not qualified. I thought he knew quite a lot about painting. He also had a large family with numerous children. We worked on painting houses and school buildings. I remember trying to paint flagpoles. That was very scary. I made a special brace and clamped it to our tallest ladder. It wrapped around the flagpole so our ladder wouldn't slip off the iron pipe. These flagpoles were quite rusty. We had to sand and scrape the old paint off. The ladders weren't tall enough, so I got an old paintbrush and taped it to a pole and climbed up the 40-foot ladder and stood on the second or third rung. I took the long pole and painted the top with the brush. We put only one coat of paint on those flagpoles. It seemed that my boss didn't want to climb the ladder, so I did. Oh boy, that was scary, with concrete below us. Later, I read the contract that my boss had with the school district. It clearly stated two coats of paint. I was upset with him and went to my pastor to get advice about what to do.

I thought about starting my own painting business. Being a contractor is not easy because your work is up and down: one day you have work, the next day you don't. About this time, there was a storm called the Columbus Day storm, which blew down trees. Gail was working at Fred Meyer grocery store on 39th Ave. and Hawthorne Blvd. The wind was so strong it blew in the glass windows at the store. My boss and I didn't have work at that time, so I went around with a chainsaw and contracted on my own, sawing trees and tree limbs. I actually hired my boss to help me. Now, I was his boss for a while. Later he moved back to West Virginia where he'd been raised. His family went first, and he moved in with us for about a week or two. I had dreams of starting my own business. I bought his Chevy van that was like a station wagon. This was a big mistake. I borrowed money from the bank to buy the van, and my friend left to go to West Virginia and join his family. I now owned his van. I drove it for about two weeks, and the engine didn't work anymore. We parked it in the front yard, out of the way. I was making payments on the van and had to have full insurance coverage. This was quite a painful experience for Gail and me. I went looking for another car to buy. I found an old Plymouth that had been restored, that they were selling cheap, for $500. This was to be one of the greatest buys I would make in my life. It ran outstandingly for a long, long time.

Another thing I like to brag about was that I saw in the Oregonian two cemetery plots for sale for only twenty-five dollars a plot. What a buy! We still have those plots today, and probably Gail and I will be buried there. I was thinking and preparing way ahead of time, you see.

Building together. The Elys really liked us and showed great support for us. We were going to their church. Our neighbors, next to our little rental house, were easy to talk to, and were very supportive of us. They had maybe 3 to 5 acres of land and had a big garden that I enjoyed looking at. The Elys let Gail and me plant a large garden. This was something I really enjoyed doing,

Along this same line, later in our life, Charles Nielsen, who was a Professor at Warner Pacific College and a dear friend, asked Gail if she would go back to college to finish her degree. She had already gone five years. She would have to go another semester. She said no, I want to help Chuck. This was what was going to happen in many ways. However, Gail and I are so different, like salt and pepper. We make everything taste better, but we're different. I would say Gail and I made music together. I remember that the Dean of the student body at Warner Pacific College, who taught different subjects, told me that Gail was one of his best students, and that if he were single, looking for a wife, he would pursue her. He was married and had children, and perhaps in his 50s. This made me feel so good.

More than a chicken coop. I went to the Elys and asked them if I could build a chicken coop. They said yes, and oh boy was I excited. One of the early days of building, Gail came out of our rental house and in her gentle way, with her eyes sparkling, said, can I help you? Wow, this woman wanted to help me. She grabbed a hammer and started pounding nails along side of me. This was outstanding. I knew I had married the girl of my dreams. Oh BOY, this was going to be my future with Gail, standing together, working together, and supporting one another for all of the future. I can't describe in words what this meant to me.

Blue bus accident. One night on the job, a strange and scary thing happened. I was there by myself, cleaning the buses as usual. I parked one of the buses. The door operated by air. I was to partially release the air, and run out of the door before the door closed. This I had done many, many times without a problem; however, as I ran to the doorway this night, the door started to close. I got my head through the door, but the door closed around my neck. There I was, stuck, but to my good fortune, there was rubber neoprene that was 3 to 4 inches wide on both sides of the door, so I didn't choke. But I was stuck, I couldn't open the door. It looked like I would spend the night there until the morning crew showed up.

I pulled with all my strength to open the door. It would not open. I wrestled with this door, pulling and pushing in all directions. The door refused to budge. This was miserable, being caught by my neck with my head outside the door. This was scary, and very uncomfortable. It seemed like I could do nothing to help myself. About an hour later, the air pressure bled down, and I could physically push the doors open. The next day, at work, I told my bosses, so we worked out a different way of closing those doors. I opened a side window, went outside, and reached in through the window and closed the door by pulling a lever. This was, by far, the safest way to close the door.

Cabinet maker. I then went to work for a cabinet maker. I was in my element of happiness, doing something that I enjoyed doing. And, of course, this furthered my abilities to build cabinets, and I was expanding my knowledge for contracting in the future. Later, when I became self-employed, I did a lot of work for the daughter of the cabinet maker who attended our church. The cabinet maker's son and his wife also attended this same church. They were well educated people, and I was more like a blue-collar worker.

Hydraulics and welding. A man I met through the church who was involved with basketball called me and asked me if I wanted to work for him in hydraulics. Dupar Dynamics was the name of the company. It seemed to me it was a step up, so I said yes. There I learned to weld and build power units that did all kinds of industrial type of work. However, I was not inclined to be a mechanic. It was hard for me to learn about hydraulics, but I did to a certain level. The only thing I liked about the job was building the crates for shipping.

CHAPTER FOUR: CHILDREN AND THE LADD'S ADDITION HOUSE

A growing family. During Gail's first pregnancy, we went back to Ohio to visit my parents. We took the train and tried to sleep in our seats, but ended up staying up all night, as I remember. I think it took three days and two nights to get to Cincinnati, Ohio. After getting back to Oregon, it wasn't long before Gail gave birth. Erma Hanson, Gail's mom, helped Gail with our newborn. His name was Timothy Dwayne Burroughs.

Erma and Howard Hanson had moved out to Oregon from Cedar Rapids, Iowa after we had been married for about six months. Gail and I were attending the Richmond Church of God in Portland, Oregon. The church asked us if we would teach a Sunday school class for the fourth graders, and we did. To our amazement, when the fourth graders became fifth-graders they promoted us, and when the fifth-graders became sixth-graders they promoted us again. By the time we taught the seventh-graders, we still had the same students, which wasn't a bad idea, having someone stay a long time with the same youth. I started playing basketball with the church league, which played at Warner Pacific College. That college had just built a new gymnasium. This was great! At one point, one of the youths from the church came to me and asked if we could form a basketball team, and I became their coach. We played other church teams in the Church of God, and that was great. The team was basically made up of the same young people as the Sunday school classes that I taught. Gail became very busy taking care of our children. I think our daughter Lynda was born about then.

Fragile babies. Babies scared me to death. I felt like they were so fragile. Just holding one, I felt like I might drop the baby, or hurt it in some way. I don't really know the cause of my fear. I had no example from my father taking care of babies or taking care of my brothers and myself. There was no real bonding with my father in my younger years. I had learned that raising babies was woman's work. I did learn differently as time went on, and I grew to have more confidence in myself.

Ladd's Addition house. When Lynda arrived, it became clear that our little one-bedroom house was not adequate. Gail pressured me to look for new housing. I was very economically motivated to improve our finances, so we started looking for a duplex. The Ladd's Addition neighborhood seemed to be a great place to buy, and the church was close by. The school system seemed to us to be great. The first house we looked at was a half a block from the school and could be converted into a duplex. However, I investigated by talking to the neighbors. It had a flat roof. I didn't like that. They said the house had had a large fire that burned off the roof, and the home was left open to the weather. So we looked at an existing duplex about four blocks away from the school. It needed a lot of work, but that didn't scare me. My mother, bless her heart, gave us $1,000 for the down payment. The Federal Housing Authority required some repair work, which I did before signing papers. This became our home for the next 38 years.

A Mrs. Curtis and her two teenage children rented the upstairs. We became landlords for the first time. Over the years we became friends with the Curtis family, helping one another. Mrs. Curtis stayed with us 32 years. At that time, the Ladd's Addition was not thought of by some as being a desirable place to live. But it was convenient for us, and the kids could walk to school. The house was a three-bedroom, one bath on the main level. As time went by, I put a bedroom in the basement, and we had bunk beds in the upstairs bedroom. I probably could have put in a second bathroom at that time, but I didn't. But before we sold the duplex, I did put in a second bathroom in the basement.

Skiing. One of the fun things that Gail and I learned to do was downhill ski. We bought a family pass for a few years and had great fun with our children. They became quite good skiers. This became a great activity for our family. I also bought a boat and took the family camping as often as we could.

One of the greatest things to happen in my life at first seemed like a disaster. In February of 1970, we had a large fire in the upstairs apartment of our home which burned off a portion of the roof and sun porch. Our third child, Ann (born in April of 1969), was a baby in her crib and just about got hit by sheetrock falling from the upstairs ceiling. We moved our renters, Mrs. Curtis and her two children, into our basement and made them as comfortable as we could. We cooked for them while we made repairs. This was extremely hard, nerve-racking and stressful, but we did it. I cashed out with the insurance company and started repairing our house by myself. I hired Howard, Gail's father, to help me. I worked nights and weekends for four months, at the same time I was working 40 hours a week in being a hydraulic mechanic. When I got the work done, the Curtis family moved back upstairs.

It could have been a disaster. One of our family vacations was to British Colombia, Canada. We went to the Campbell River, and camped and fished. This is a story of a close call, almost a tragic accident. One day, Gail and I took the children out fishing. We stored our boat next to a logging company which would float logs beside where we docked our boat. I got carried away and stayed too long out on the river, and it was getting dark. I needed to get back to the dock, but I was catching fish, and it was hard to pull up anchor when I was still catching fish. It was almost dark, so I pulled up anchor, started the 25-horsepower motor and headed for the dock. What I didn't know was the logging company had moved a bunch of logs very close to where we were to dock our boat. I didn't see the logs, and we drove the boat up on the logjam. Everyone stayed in the boat. The boat didn't tip over because I hit the logjam head on, not sideways. What good fortune with small children in the boat. We all had life preservers on. Nobody got hurt. A worker with a small boat came to our rescue and we were able to pull the boat off the logjam. We often thought about what might have happened – that "what if" factor.

Gail never did like boating or water outings like I did. I was always sad about not taking more camping trips and boating trips. You see, when I became self-employed, work became the main focus of my life, work and more work with no time to play.

Dupar Dynamics. At this time a recession was going on, and workers were getting laid off. My shop had 18 workers. However, they were laying off workers, and now there were only three people left working in the shop. Let me take this time to explain how difficult it was working there. The worst thing that could happen to you was to be promoted to a leadership role, such as foreman. This was because the workers tried their best to get rid of the leader, so they could be promoted, and I experienced a new foreman about every six months. Before the recession, Dupar Dynamics merged with another hydraulics company, and our bosses became workers with their bosses becoming our bosses. You can see why that might not work. Some of the office managers went out and started their own hydraulic business, taking some of our customers away.

There were five new hydraulic companies started from the discontent from the Dupar Dynamics merger. I couldn't find another job in hydraulics. All the companies in the Portland area were laying off, not hiring. I applied at many different types of jobs. I didn't care what they were, I needed to find work.

Dirty tricks. This leads me to a bad experience I had. One of my foremen, knowing that he was going to quit and go with a new company and take some of our customers with him, guided me in building some hydraulic power units, giving me, on purpose, wrong information about how I was going to build these units; and, of course, I built them wrong. I got all the blame when that foreman left. I knew what had happened and why he did what he did. It was a dirty trick, but there really was a recession going on while our company was fighting within ourselves, which only hurt everybody. One day, the new foreman and I got into a fight and I quit, and the foreman laid me off at the same time. Later, the managers of the company tried to get me to come back and work for them. I said "no," not knowing what I was going to do next.

To my amazement, people who had watched me rebuild my house after the fire called me to do repair work at their homes. It was a variety of jobs - roofing, painting, dry rot jobs, and, before I knew it, I had work lined up for a month or so. I quit looking for work in hydraulics and became a general contractor, self-employed, which was great for me. I had to learn how to bid, and how to organize this kind of work, and of course, there was a genius about me in this area of work. I could close the door to my office and take time to think it through. I learned and became very self-confident, and I always seemed to have work. People seemed to trust me and like me, so I was off and running for the next 45 years of self- employment. To my amazement, at one point I became a millionaire.

PART THREE: CHURCH INFLUENCES

••

CHAPTER ONE: YOUTH COUNSELLING AND THE CHURCH

....

A good time at church. Aside from my family, the church was where my heart was, with teaching Sunday school class and coaching basketball. The youth counselor for teenagers resigned, and Rev. Ely started looking for a new youth counselor. He told me later that he put out a fleece: that is, he prayed that God would show him who that was to be.

I thought I could be a youth counselor, even though I was still in counseling myself. I was beginning to understand how my disabilities were impacting my life and I was still figuring out how to deal with everything. The youth were the same kids that I was teaching in Sunday school class, starting at the fourth grade. I got so caught up in trying to help these teenagers become adults and be good Christians. Why was I chosen to do this when I was trying to work through my past? Of course, it was a volunteer position. I also got to serve on the board of Christian education. Sometimes, I spent more than 40 hours a week for the church, plus worked a 40-hour day job. I can remember Gail complaining, with good cause, that I was spending too much time for the church, and not helping much with our own children. This was true, but she loved me, and I loved her, so we worked through this time. I was a youth counselor for five years, and also continued to coach basketball. Sometimes I taught Sunday school class. This was a very busy time. It was also the most successful thing I'd ever done for the church, and Gail and I were enriched beyond words. I still keep in contact with some of those youth, who now are in their 60s, and their parents. We also kept busy with various other activities and outings with the church.

A sign from God? I pulled into a gas station to get gas for my car, and a perfect stranger came up to me and asked for help. His wife was having an affair with another man. I told him that I was not a counselor, and he should go to see my pastor, and he did. To my amazement, during that week, I had two other total strangers ask me if I could help them with counseling for their marriage. I sent them to Rev. Ely. They all three went, which is also amazing. According to Rev. Ely, this was the answer that God had picked me to be the new youth counselor. Oh boy, this was exciting, but scary.

We became very close friends with a couple who attended the Richmond church. We played cards together, probably once a week. I also started hunting and fishing with this friend. This would become a 45-year relationship: Words cannot describe our pleasure to have such close friends. The

Richmond Church years were a time of making very close friendships which have continued over many, many, years.

Gail and I took the youth group to the beach twice a year. We camped at Cape Lookout in tents during the summertime. Then, in the fall, we rented motel rooms at Netarts, Oregon. When doing outdoor camping I can remember taking six mill plastic, very thick, and building a large tent so that many of the kids could stay together. We roasted hot dogs, and the kids loved to give me burnt hot dogs. I would eat and eat way more than I should have.

The youth group brought out some of my outstanding skills. I was a great organizer, and a person who took care of small details to make sure everything went well. I pretty much followed the teachings of the church, as the Christian education board gave me materials to follow. I also brought in a lot of parents to teach the group because some of the parents were professors at Warner Pacific College. I was still trying my best to accept the teachings of the Church of God.

One of the girls in the youth group who was the youth president was extremely brilliant and challenged me all the time. She told me one time that I didn't know exactly what I believed about God. She was seeking a deeper understanding than I could provide her. This was on an educational level, not accepting the teachings of the church by feelings, emotions, or experiences. I was operating on an experience of life level, not a college level of theology, so she turned to pastors and professors to seek this level of understanding, which I felt was okay. But I was also seeking to know theology, and my experience with her inspired me, later in life, to seek to know theology on a college level.

Heart-breaking. Life has a way of breaking your heart. Rev. Ely had an enlarged heart. The doctors advised him to have open heart surgery, which he did, and he died on the operating table. I think there were about 500 people in the congregation. They selected a new pastor and the congregation dwindled down to 10 families or 20 people.

Gail and I resigned as youth counselors. They asked me to teach the college-age Sunday school class, which were again the same kids I taught when they were fourth graders. I didn't feel qualified, but I did it anyway. I didn't think I had enough education. We muddled through that year.

A difficult time. At this time. I still didn't know the extent of my disability. I had never been tested for dyslexia or a hearing problem. My reading skills had now grown to probably a seventh-grade level, so working for the church seemed to me to be the right thing to do. I felt that God had called me to be the youth counselor and Sunday school teacher over the years at Richmond church.

But I did not like the new pastor, as he preached in favor of the Vietnam War. He also wanted to buy up housing around the Richmond church without a congregational vote, just the Board of Trustee's approval. These two things were too much for me. The youth group started to dwindle down. I offered to be youth counselor again and the church said no.

In some ways this would turn out to be the best for me and Gail.

Brothers and sisters. There was something else that happened during our time at Richmond that gave me a lasting negative feeling towards the church. This may not seem much, but to me it was a big deal. I had a habit of calling my fellow church peers "brother" and "sister". This made me feel like we were a close family of Christian believers. A couple from the church scolded me and said he was not my brother and she was not my sister. I began to realize a separation between the adult members. I quit calling my fellow church members brother and sister and bonding with other Christians. I must admit that the family feeling of support and unity among the church members went away.

During that time in the early 1960s, Wade resigned as pastor of Holladay Park Church of God and went to work for suicide prevention. He also had a private counseling clientele and worked with Youth for Christ. I met him for counseling in the Youth for Christ office. He was into horses, camping and guide service. I went with him on a horseback outing to a camp he had on Mount Jefferson. This was great fun. To my sadness, he died in an accident. He jumped off a hayloft into his truck, fell backwards and hit his head on a bumper and died. I lost a friend and my counselor, so I was on my own. It would be about 10 years before I would see a counselor again.

CHAPTER TWO: HOLLADAY PARK AND TIGARD CHURCHES OF GOD-

···

Obsessive-compulsive disorder (OCD) is a mental illness that causes repeated unwanted thoughts or sensations (obsessions) or the urge to do something over and over again (compulsions). Some people can have both obsessions and compulsions. OCD isn't about habits like biting your nails or thinking negative thoughts. An obsessive thought might be that certain numbers or colors are "good" or "bad." A compulsive habit might be to wash your hands seven times after touching something that could be dirty. Although you may not want to think or do these things, you feel powerless to stop. People with OCD have thoughts or actions that: take up at least an hour a day; are beyond their control; aren't enjoyable; and/or interfere with work, social life or other aspects of one's daily routine. Many people who have OCD know that their thoughts and habits don't make sense. They don't do them because they enjoy them, but because they can't quit. And if they stop, they feel so bad that they start again. There isn't a cure for OCD; but a combination of treatments, including medicine, psychotherapy, meditation, and Transcranial Magnetic Stimulation, that can help to manage symptoms.

- *WebMD*

It was very difficult for me to change churches from a church that allowed me to be a leader, Sunday school teacher and youth counselor for over 14 years. I was in a foreign country, so to speak. Most of the Richmond Church congregation who left the church went over to the Woodstock Church of God. I couldn't stand the evangelistic preaching there. At Holladay Park, the pastor didn't preach that way. So that is why we chose Holladay Park Church. At that time Holladay Park had about 300 or more attending church.

Holladay Park Church. We attended Holladay Park Church of God for about eight years. These were hard years: I had started my business, and had to learn how to be self-employed, the ups and downs of being a contractor, and the transition from Richmond Church of God, where I was given leadership roles. Now, that was gone. I thought that I was called to be a teacher of a Sunday school class. It was hard for me to adjust to a new situation. This church had a segment of blue-collar workers. However, college professors, doctors, and professional people ran the church. I probably, in reality, had no complaints. I started a youth basketball team, and was asked to serve on the building committee, which I did. The pastor did not preach in an evangelistic style, but he seemed to have a knack, they said, for raising money. About 200 people attended every Sunday. Gail and I attended a Sunday school class for adults.

I'm afraid that lots of my frustration and negativity came out in this transition. Our daughter Lynda and son Tim were teenagers at this time; Ann was younger. I was working six days a week, and Gail started working with me. I really wasn't happy because I hadn't resolved how I was raised, and still felt guilty all the time about everything, wanting everything to be perfect, and of course, it was not. Tim and Ann seemed to do well at church, but Lynda rebelled, it seemed to me, very hard. She wouldn't accept our guidance or authority, and, quite frankly, I didn't know how to guide her. She was a very independent girl whom we loved, but she went her own way regardless of what Gail or I said. Lynda painted an arrow on her bedroom wall pointing outward and declared her desire to be free of her parents. She also had a big influence on Ann, saying things that teenagers say and probably regret later.

We had been attending Holladay Park Church for about six or seven years when I got into trouble emotionally. I started thinking about the second work of grace, where you're supposed to receive the Holy Spirit. Gail's father, Howard, was preaching to me about this. He accused us of being sinful, and about watching too much TV. I had my first bout of serious OCD (Obsessive-Compulsive Disorder) thinking about sanctification. I started to think about it day and night and every waking moment. I would think about it over and over in my mind; it would not stop. I was contracting and working very hard at various jobs. I was not sleeping at night thinking over and over again about this theological doctrine of the Church of God. My sleeping pattern was that I could not go to sleep at night for two nights, then the third night I would sleep extremely hard and long, then the next two nights I couldn't sleep, then the third night I would die, so to speak, and sleep very hard. This went on with me for one year. I was barely functioning, carrying out my life as best I could, crawling out of bed, going to work, and trying to be a parent. I became very depressed, and I needed to do something to change this pattern. I don't know what Gail thought. She seemed to be there as best she could. It was up to me to bite the bullet and seek help. The church was of no help because I would talk to the pastor about the second work, or sanctification, and of course he supported it, but never preached it from the pulpit. This didn't stop my think-ing over and over about what the church said. I didn't neces-sarily agree with the teaching, and yet I was attending this church, and Gail's father Howard kept teaching me I was evil, but I tried to ignore him. I knew a professor who taught at Warner Pacific College, who had retired. She had taught psy-chology and was a preacher. I asked Gail to go with me and ask her if she would counsel me, to help me with my OCD and depression. To my amazement, she said yes. She told me she was depressed also, and that we could work on it to-gether, that she and I would try to free ourselves from de-pression.

The book *Feeling Good*. I was driving in my car listening to a radio program that talked about a new book called *Feeling Good,* by David Burns. I took this book to my new counselor and she said let's work on this together. She did things differently. I would meet with her and talk as long as I wanted to, sometimes as long as three hours at a time. Most of the time, we delved into my past for about two hours, how I was raised, about my parents, and how I could forgive them. And, little by little, I got better. She also prayed with me that my business would be successful. I felt like I was failing at that time; yet, to my amazement, I landed eight Sears retail store remodels. I also worked for FMC Corporation remodeling offices, and there I met a man who would work together with me on commercial projects. He was an engineer who did drafting work for me. I built a christening platform for an oil tanker, and Governor Tom McCall of Oregon and his wife came down from Salem and christened the oil tanker, built by FMC Corporation.

I landed a Memorial Coliseum job where I remodeled the food canteens and built the food carts. It seemed to me that my prayers were being answered. I was getting better and better. My OCD left me; I stopped thinking about the second work of grace, and my depression was lifted about this time.

My father passed away in 1987. At his funeral I said nice things about him. I felt that emotionally I had turned a great corner and was on my way again. Depression was always around at different times, but not overwhelming me. I heard about people taking a magic pill that relieved them from depression, but I never sought help from my medical provider at that time.

Praying. There were lots of times that I prayed and there was no answer. I would ask the question: Why was I depressed all the time? Why didn't God heal me? I don't know. There are times that we pray and there are answers, meaning what we pray for comes true. I prayed, and my counselor prayed, and things did come true. I do not think that when you pray and nothing happens, that you have done something wrong and that God is not listening. I believe God gives good gifts to all who pray, but I don't know, and maybe I don't need to know, why some things are not answered in the way we want them to be answered. In the years to come, I would continue to suffer a great deal with OCD and depression.

My days at Holladay Park were numbered. The pastor resigned, and one of the members of the church said he felt called to take the pastor's place. Some people believed in him, so they hired him. He was very evangelistic, and he told the congregation they were sinners and needed to rededicate their lives to Jesus.

Tigard Church of God. One time, at Holladay Park Church of God, on a youth church bus outing, some boys pulled some clothes off our girls. I don't think it went very far. But after that, Gail and I started looking for a new church. Our son Tim was actually attending two churches, Vancouver

Church of God, and Holladay Park. Lynda didn't want to attend any church at that time, and Ann didn't want to attend church either. Gail and I chose to attend Tigard Church of God.

We liked the pastor's preaching at Tigard. We also liked the youth pastor. He had gentle and compassionate ways. It was just right for our daughters. Gail and I attended Tigard Church of God for the next 14 years. They were good years, but I was up and down with my depression. A couple from this church, who had been missionaries to Costa Rica, became good friends to us.

Costa Rica. A group of us from the Tigard church went to Costa Rica to build a church, and to do other projects. We were allowed to bring only two bags each for boarding the plane. Thank goodness many people only brought one suitcase, as I loaded nine suitcases full of tools, screws, and nails that I thought we needed to complete our task. The visit was very difficult, as much of the preparation work was not done for us ahead of time. When we got to Costa Rica, we found out that the land had not yet been purchased for us to build the church. So, we were given small jobs around already existing churches and a parsonage, such as building kitchen cabinets and pouring concrete sidewalks and hanging doors in the parsonage. All these things needed to be done, including a lot of painting of existing buildings. We also did a lot of sightseeing and enjoyed the fellowship of the group.

A retired missionary asked me if I would serve on the missionary board at the Tigard church, which I did. They supported me, and they asked me if I would represent the Tigard church in starting a homeless shelter program, which I was excited to do. They say fools rush in where angels fear to tread, and oh my, this was a big mistake on my part. I did this work for about two years, and this was a bad decision for my personal life. I was taking a night course for dyslexic adults to learn how to read and write better. I worked at this very hard. I also had an 80 hour per week self-employed contracting job to take care of, and a wife and teenagers, and now, the demands of wanting to show the world that I was capable of a leadership role in the church.

Homeless shelter difficulty. The city of Tigard did need a homeless shelter, a place for people to go. The leader of our meetings was helping, spending extraordinary hours to make the shelter program work. This program required more of my time than I had to give, so I gave up the reading and writing program for dyslexics. The leader of the shelter program would not allow our meetings to be recorded, and would not appoint a treasurer, and yet she went out to the churches and the community and asked for money and support. I had organized our church to help. I stayed overnight different nights to help with the homeless program and asked our church for money. I stood up against the leader and asked her to record the meetings and to appoint a treasurer. I asked for support from other volunteers who represented different churches. I was not able to accomplish this. When I reported back to my missionary board, it seemed to me, I got no support. The Tigard church would not take a stand against the leader and said that they would have to take over the shelter program. They did not want Gail or me to do that anymore. It also seemed to me that there was a certain amount of blame cast on me for not being a desirable leader. This, of course, was the opposite of what I was trying to accomplish. I lost big time, and I resigned. I found another person to lead this program for our church who asked me to stay on for six months to a year, which I did. And, of course, I worried and worried and worried, for my OCD bothered me a great deal.

About two years later, there was a write-up in the Tigard newspaper saying this director was no longer in charge of the shelter program. The city mayor and council took over the program and the director of the shelter program left town. They wanted to do an audit to see if she stole any money. There were no records of how much money was collected, but I felt vindicated. I sent the article to our pastor.

I knew that my time trying to be a volunteer in any leadership roles had come and gone. So, I concentrated on being the best contractor that I could; I made work the most important thing in my life, plus trying to be a good husband, and a good father to my family. I accepted just sitting in the pew, although this was such a huge disappointment in my life. It seemed to me that the church had created more problems for me in my life than it had helped me. I became resentful of the church, and more aware of the huge problems of doctrine in the Church of God. I tried my best to not address these, and not support them either, but to just ignore them.

CHAPTER THREE: BUILDING HOUSES (WHILE SUFFERING)

....

Ménière's Disease (MD) *is a disorder of the inner ear that is characterized by episodes of severe vertigo (feeling like the world is spinning), and/or ringing in the ears (tinnitus), hearing loss, and fullness in the ear. Typically, only one ear is initially affected; however, over time both ears may become involved. Episodes generally last from 20 minutes to a few hours. The time between episodes varies. The hearing loss and ringing in the ears can become constant over time.*

The cause of Ménière's disease is unclear but likely involves both genetic and environmental factors. A number of theories exist for the causes of Meniere's, including constriction in blood vessels, viral infections, and autoimmune reactions. About 10% of cases run in families. Symptoms are believed to occur as the result of increased fluid build-up in the labyrinth of the inner ear. Diagnosis is based on the symptoms and, frequently, a hearing test is suggested. Other conditions that may produce similar symptoms include vestibular migraine and transient ischemic attack.

A cure does not exist. Attacks are often treated with medications to help with nausea and anxiety. Measures to prevent attacks are overall poorly supported by the evidence. A low-salt diet, diuretics, and corticosteroids may be tried. Physical therapy may help with balance and counselling may help with anxiety. Injections into the ear or surgery may also be tried if other measures are not effective, but are associated with risks. The use of tympanostomy tubes, while popular, is not supported.

It most often starts in people 40 to 60 years old. After 5 to 15 years of symptoms, the episodes of the world spinning generally stop and the person is left with mild loss of balance, moderately poor hearing in the affected ear, and ringing in the ear.

-   Wikipedia

G ail and I realized that we could not continue working physically as hard as we were doing. And we were just paying the bills and not saving much. I knew we had to change what and how we were conducting our contracting business. At the same time, we were doing the Sears remodels, and a friend was still helping us with bidding and doing those jobs.

A couple we had met at the Richmond Church of God approached me and asked me if I would consider building houses. This couple were home builders who worked side by side. They also liked to teach others how to build houses. By this time, I had been in business for 25 years and had done almost everything to our house that could be done. I'd built outward and upward and downward, and had done all kinds of repairs. I had built fences and decks; you name it, I had done it. However, I had not built a house from the ground up. These friends were millionaires. It was scary to change and try something totally different. They wanted to teach us their way of success and how to build a house. This couple had watched me be a youth counselor, and the success that I had there. So, we had meetings with them and decided to start a new adventure and build houses. We bought their blueprints and followed their guidance and built our first house. We sold our first house to a couple who were choir directors at the Tigard Church of God where we were attending at the time. We made a good profit, and so off we went into building houses. Gail and I were hands-on people, so we took what they presented us, and changed some things to accommodate the way we liked to do things. We discovered that we could not duplicate their profit. They did everything they could to cut costs to the extreme, I thought. And they sold their houses cheaper than anyone could, and still made a profit.

I think we built about 50 houses over 10 years and did very well financially. During this time, I bought land that I could subdivide into many lots, and built many houses, and a triplex, which I wanted to keep. My son Tim, who was a paramedic, would come on his days off and help Gail and me build houses. We all learned a great deal from each other. Tim had worked for a framer, and so eventually he would frame up my houses by himself. Gail and Tim and I would pour the foundations; then, Tim would frame up the houses.

Unbelievable publicity. An amazing thing happened - *The Oregonian* newspaper came out to interview Gail and me and wrote an article about us. It was printed for all of Portland to read, all of the newspaper's subscribers. This was astonishing and amazing. It made me so proud of who we were and what we were about.

A subdivision nightmare. I purchased a new subdivision from ODOT, Oregon Department of Transportation, which was North of Division St. and 96th Ave. I was so proud of myself that I was able to purchase this property, but it would be my Waterloo, so to speak. A person called me on the phone to inform me that the street in front of this property had been a major highway and had over twelve inches to two feet of concrete underneath the black top, and I would need to run the sewer line there, and this would cost me a great deal of money.

When I went to the Portland city building department to investigate, the woman who helped me told me that I would be very, very sorry that I bought this property, and that running the sewer would probably bankrupt me. Also, Tim, my son, informed me that he was taking a job with the Church of God to run a camp, called Camp White Branch, near the Mackenzie River. Before buying this property, I was having major health problems with dizziness and vertigo where I couldn't even walk without difficulty. This would come and go. I was seeing doctors who told me I had Ménière's disease, and they didn't know what caused it, or how to treat it.

So, there were days I couldn't go to work. My OCD kicked in, and I worried and worried and worried about this problem of running a sewer line in front of this subdivision. There were days I was lying in bed, not able to walk, read, or watch TV. The room was spinning, and I was worried sick. The days that I could work, I laid out my houses and triplex, divided up the land into lots, applied for building permits, and hired a surveyor to lay out the lots. I started working on what and who could do the sewer work, and sought someone who could give me prices. I realized I did not have the knowledge or experience to handle these problems. The vertigo was getting worse. With my OCD, I started thinking day and night, every hour, every minute of the day and night, how I was going to solve these problems. I had gone into overload, and my emotions were shot. I became very, very sick.

Despite all the challenges, I always tried to handle things in a strong, unemotional way. I started counseling again, with someone who, I thought, also needed my help. He was going through a divorce, and also needed clients. So, we helped each other. I needed to take care of my health and reduce the problems that were creating my OCD. I had always thought I would be strong enough to handle these kinds of issues. But I had to give up and sell the property that I had developed into a subdivision. It was unthinkable. There was money and profit to be made and I should carry on, but I was still sick with Ménière's disease. Ten days out of each month I couldn't walk, or eat; I would vomit up my meals. I was extremely sick, and I needed help. I talked with the mentors who helped us get into house building. The only advice they had for me was that they were maybe willing to buy the property and give us only what I paid for the land. I couldn't sell them the property right away because I had developed the property, paid for the building permits, and had more money into it than they would pay me. But I was sick, very sick. I shared with them that I was seeing a counselor, and that I had Ménière's disease. I was an entrepreneur. I wouldn't sell this property for a loss. How could I be true to myself and do this? I was between a rock and a very hard place. Also, how could I sell them a piece of property that might lose them money if they had to run the sewer line?

Oh, what agony and misery I was in. The building permits were almost ready to be picked up. To my good fortune, I found a sewer contractor who had worked in the street before and said that there would be no problem; he gave me a price that was very reasonable, so the properties or subdivision would be profitable. But I still had the OCD that would not quit every minute of every day and night. I was thinking about these problems as if I had not yet solved them. How could I stop the OCD and get relief, and get a good night's sleep, to take this burden off me? My "mentor" builders saw a way to make a profit from this job. I must say, I was grateful for their help at first, when I first started building houses. So, I made the unthinkable decision to sell to them this subdivision for what I had paid for the land and the building permits.

Surgery on my ear. The exact cause for Ménière's Disease is not known. It may be due to moisture building up next to your eardrum that cannot be absorbed by your body. Professionals will not do surgery until you are practically deaf. Well, I became deaf, down to 3% hearing in my right ear. They cut out the bone around my ear to provide more surface for the water to be absorbed. The surgery was successful and slowly the vertigo problem went away, and my OCD went away.

This was a very, very hard time for me and Gail. We had lost a large sum of money taking care of these problems. Being self-employed, you still have to pay the bills, even though you can't work during your illness.

I still built a few houses and got into building small apartments. This meant I could stop thinking about this property. It would take a long while, but eventually I quit thinking about it.

We met another couple who were the new people our building mentors were teaching how to build houses. They had been ministers for many years in Colorado. When I was in the hospital after my surgery, they came and visited me, trying to be friends and comforting me emotionally. I will always be grateful to them.

The remodel. Gail and I decided to remodel our home on Elliott Ave. in Portland, Oregon in the Ladd's Addition. This home, as I mentioned earlier, was an up and down duplex. Mrs. Curtis, who lived above us, was an extremely nice lady, but she was in her 80s, climbing a set of stairs. I thought we would ask her to leave during this remodel. She did, and she moved into a high-rise apartment with an elevator near the Lloyd Center. She also received government assistance, so financially it was a good deal for her.

Gail and I started this huge remodel in a big way. We had installed two new furnaces, air conditioners, and hot water heaters. We had a new forty-year roof installed with total removal of the old roof, with new plywood sheeting. Also, we remodeled two new kitchens with new appliances, new plumbing, and new electrical work done. Then we rented the upstairs out to new people. Oregon law makes it hard on landlords. Whoever shows up with the money can rent the apartment. The landlord does not have a choice. These new renters were Reed College girls who needed a place to live, and we accepted them. They were difficult to deal with. They were very noisy. They were smart, and selfish, and Gail had trouble dealing with these girls. I did too, but we muddled through with them. When they left, we again rented it out, this time to Lewis and Clark college girls. They had the money, and by law we could not deny them.

At some point, Gail wanted to sell this duplex that we had lived in for 38 years. The building was now 100 years old. It took us nine months to sell the duplex. This was very emotional, and brought us a lot of heartache. We then moved into one of our rental buildings that we had recently remodeled. It was a cracker box in the Lentz district, and had two bedrooms, two bathrooms, with a one car garage. We started looking for our new home.

Our new home. It seems to me that it took about a year to find our new home in a beautiful location in Happy Valley, Oregon. We bought it from a couple we knew through the Church of God. It was a fixer-upper, built on a half-acre in the 50s, needing a huge amount of work. It has a view of five mountains, which was the reason we bought it. We could see Mt. Hood, Mt. St. Helens, Mt. Adams, Mt. Rainier, and a peak of Mt. Jefferson; plus, it had a park-like setting with lots of flowers, and rhododendron trees that provided a great deal of beauty. That's what we wanted. It had space for a huge garden, which was a must for me. I thought we could do a remodel in about a year, but it took two years for the big stuff to be done, and another two years to finish the job. This was an exciting time for us. I love to do construction and remodel work, and it was enjoyable for Gail and me to completely rebuild a home, add about 1000 sq. ft., build a new attached garage with a storage loft and oversized space. We put in a retaining wall out of large rocks down below, to help flatten out an area for a garden. We raised the ground about 3 feet. We put in a new water sprinkler system and planted new trees and lawn.

There seems to be, in life, always a hard place. And this work was emotionally and physically draining for me; I became exhausted doing much of the work myself. So Gail helped, and we hired our son, Tim, to help us. Everything was going great, and I felt emotionally good about what we were doing. I hired a surveyor to survey our property and found that people on all sides didn't know where the property lines were.

Damage done by just seven feet. After the property survey, we found that our property line went into the property below us by about 7 feet. Everyone thought the old retaining wall was the property line, but our property actually extended past this old retaining wall.

This, of course, was very upsetting to the property owner below us. I talked with her and asked her not to pay the lawyers a great deal of money to deal with this. I also turned to my lawyer, which was a mistake. He told me that I would not lose this property of 7 feet in the back, and that no way could she take it from me. He asked if he could write a letter to her, and he did, and to my amazement this started a legal battle with her. This was very upsetting. After a few meetings with my lawyer, he admitted that he was not knowledgeable in this area of the law, and that he'd started me down the wrong road. My next lawyer told me I would lose, but I wanted some money for this property that I was going to lose. To make a long story short, the property owner down below would not pay me any money, but would spend it on lawyers. She was going to take me to court, which was going to cost thousands and thousands of dollars. I gave in, and gave her the 7 feet, and made the property line the old retaining wall, and lost a lot of money on lawyers. Because of the cost and emotional turmoil, along with my OCD during the heat of the battle, I became very depressed.

Counselors. This was to be the deepest depression of my life. I turned to my health care provider. This was a big mistake.

My counselor was very professional, but I knew that she disagreed with the drugs that the psychiatrist was prescribing. My HMO put me in a program called Mindfulness, and told me to practice this for a great deal of my time. I did this for three hours a day, only to get worse and worse. This sent me into a deep depression. Finally, I had a total breakdown. They pulled me out of Mindfulness and recommended that I be hospitalized. My counselor quit her job over what had happened to me. I think she was protesting what they had done to me. I went off to a 10-day treatment at the hospital in Salem, Oregon, which was awful. I was very suicidal, delusional, and extremely depressed with my OCD working all the time against me. Salem's doctors immediately took me off of the HMO's drugs and put me on totally different drugs. The teachers were not skilled in teaching this Mindfulness program the right way. They didn't put any limitations of time on practicing this program. Later, I learned that I should have only been doing this for 15 to 20 minutes a day, not three to four hours a day. My therapist had not considered my OCD. I have always been an all-out personality because I wanted to get better. But in this case, this was totally wrong for me. Eventually, I had to forgive them for leading me astray.

It would take about two years of my life to get back to where I was emotionally. I was managing my depression and OCD fairly well at times and didn't need experimental drugs. The drugs that my HMO put me on also took away some of my ability to remember the past. It's like wiping your memory bank clean in some areas. I now relied on Gail for help. And after ten days of being locked up in a mental hospital, I had to withdraw from very strong drugs, which I did slowly, and with painful side effects. My family now knows that I struggle with mental issues. Some long-time friends of ours knew, and my wife knew, that I could have committed suicide, and I was close, very close to doing this to myself. My relationships with everybody seemed to change, but I needed to get better, and it was up to me to rebuild my life.

HMO still isn't helping. After getting off the drugs, I still sought counseling at my HMO; however, I had a new counselor. His job was to get rid of me, and he told me so in a roundabout way. I'm sure the medical center was losing money on me. So, the new counselor was worthless as far as helping me. I started thinking about my past counselors and the books that I had read that helped me, so I dwelled on these. I knew that I had to get away from that place, for they totally hurt me, and almost cost me my life. We also needed to change churches. And, I needed to find a new counselor, so I went searching for someone.

I had neighbors who were good people, but I thought they were upset with Gail and me over the property line business. I started a program to help them by giving them gifts from my garden and developing a relationship of communication and friendliness towards them. We turned around our relationship with two of the neighbors, but not the one below us. She also had emotional problems and lived like a hermit; you hardly ever saw her. From my garden I gave her vegetables that I laid on her front porch; I would call her on the phone to let her know that they were there. She thanked me, but that was it.

I asked my son Tim if we could find counselors on the computer that I could consider, which he did for me. I eventually found a counselor, and slowly I was being restored. I started downhill skiing on Mt. Hood again, which I loved. I needed to increase pleasure and fun in my life. I loved to play cards, so we asked our daughter Lynda and her husband if we could cook a meal for her and play cards together once a week. For me, this broke the cycle of thinking about any problems that my OCD would concentrate on. Spending an evening with them helped me for a while. We thought they enjoyed having us, but once a week was too much for us to intrude on their lives. We had over-extended our welcome. So, we stopped going once a week. I missed this, of course. We told Bryon and Lynda we would come out to their place when we were invited. By this time, I was back on my feet again, and was maybe 80% restored, although I still had OCD and I still had depression. Our remodel had been completed, and we started looking for a new church to help rebuild my life. The Presbyterians had not answered my search for God in a doctrinal way. I also felt I should start being aggressive with my desires to find answers.

CHAPTER FOUR: QUESTIONING CHURCH DOCTRINE

···

Depression *is a mood disorder that causes a persistent feeling of*
sadness and loss of interest. Also called major depressive disorder or
clinical depression, it affects how you feel, think and behave and can
lead to a variety of emotional and physical problems. You may have
trouble doing normal day-to-day activities, and sometimes you may
feel as if life isn't worth living.

More than just a bout of the blues, depression isn't a weakness,
and you can't simply "snap out" of it. Depression may require long-
term treatment. Most people with depression feel better with medica-
tion, psychotherapy or both. For many people with depression, symp-
toms usually are severe enough to cause noticeable problems in day-
to-day activities, such as work, school, social activities or relation-
ships with others. Some people may feel generally miserable or un-
happy, without really knowing why.

\- *The Mayo Clinic*

My grandmother was a Methodist, so Gail and I started visiting the Methodist churches, and found one that seemed to be right for us. But I still had many questions. In attending, we found people that seemed to accept us. There was a men's group that was very open to discussing various subjects. They introduced me to books written by Marcus Borg.

They also were open to discussing different theories and views on doctrinal issues. I thought I had found a church where I could be myself and grow spiritually. However, Gail and I attended a small adult Sunday school class taught by a teacher who was trained, and had graduated from college, I think, with a doctorate in theology. This group welcomed me. I had different views and questions that I asked, but the teacher was closed minded, and was not open to discussing theology from the different perspective of other theologians I had read. So, my ideas got me into trouble. Gail and I withdrew from attending that class. To my amazement, many members came to me and asked me to return, but I did not want to be disruptive to the class, so I said no. The teacher was very, very upset with me, but I had a great relationship with the pastor, and with many of the men in our breakfast class, and was making deep friendships, I thought.

The church picnic. This Methodist church did not have an annual picnic, so I asked the pastor if I could start organizing church picnics. He said yes, but he predicted that not many would attend. Well, I went about organizing the picnic for our church to be held at my home. I built sawhorses for tables. I also bought a keyboard so we could have music and singing. I built a horseshoe backstop and brought in sand so we could play horseshoes at the picnic. I also rewired our outside plug-ins for keeping food hot. We had a huge turn-out. For the first two picnics I paid for everything, so for the third one I asked for donations. It did not really cover my cost. I decided to try to involve church people to form a committee for the picnic. I also knew that I needed to be flexible for changes. So I asked in church for volunteers to help me with that third picnic, incorporating other people's ideas. The pastor asked me to come to Council meeting to talk about the picnic, and have the church incorporate the cost of the picnic.

Backstabbing. I went to the Church Council meeting with a good write-up about the picnic, and tried to show that I was flexible and worthy of this endeavor. But apparently there were those who were my enemies. I had assumed that I had the support of the majority for this activity, which I think I did; but there were two or three people against me, and those people hurt me a great deal. To my amazement, I was blind-sided and fired with nobody standing up for me, including the pastor and some of my close friends. I truly didn't understand. A lady on the church committee was the one who fired me. After the meeting I asked her if we could talk. She didn't want to and shunned me. I was devastated by her reply. I decided to try to hold my head up high and reach out in fellowship with the people who had done this evil thing to me. I continued to attend the church for a while. But my OCD started working overtime, and I became very depressed. I told myself, over and over and over again, that the rejection of the church picnic was not my fault. This helped, but when you suffer from OCD, things do not go away. It probably took a year, maybe two, for me to quit thinking about the church picnic. I mean, I thought about it every day for over a year. What a battle I had inside me trying not to blame myself for what happened.

My mind became a whirlwind of uncontrollable thoughts. I could not continue to attend this church. I blamed myself very, very severely. I thought of all my mistakes in this church, and how I might have done things differently by not volunteering to do anything. I knew, deep down inside, that I hadn't done anything wrong except ask questions about doctrinal issues. How could people call themselves Christian and do such evil to me? How could I square my belief in God and his guidance with Christians who were so hurtful to me? I needed to accept their rejection and move on with my life. I needed to stop thinking about it, but this was not easy for me to do. My mind had been programmed to think and think and think about problems I encountered. I became terribly depressed. Oh my, how could I rise above this?

A man who became my friend in this church told me it was not my fault. He was totally disgusted and upset with the church, and these so-called Christians. I told him not to get involved and to let it go, that this church really needed him. He was the church treasurer, and also ran the Wednesday breakfast for the men, which was so great. I can't describe how wonderful this men's group was to me. My actions from then on out were very commendable.

Looking for a new church – again. I started looking for a new church to attend. I believed there is a God, and that men run churches. Therefore, we must separate churches from God, and realize that, many times, people in churches do not do God's will, but do great harm to one another.

I started skiing twice a week to break the thinking cycle of my OCD. A college professor friend of mine, whom I had known in the Church of God, was now attending a United Church of Christ. This church is noted for accepting people of different faiths and different lifestyles. They are noted for promoting justice, accepting a wide variety of backgrounds of religious faiths, and you could talk about any theological doctrine and they wouldn't kick you out of church like the Methodists did. Perhaps I could find a place to worship God and explore different ways of thinking. I had, finally, completely rejected "holiness" churches.

PART FOUR: THREE WONDERFUL CHILDREN

••

INTRODUCTION

··

The earlier part of this book focuses on my life and my challenges. I have mentioned our children many times, as they are, indeed, a huge part of our lives. No story of my life would be complete without a special focus on each of my three children.

How does one write about three wonderful children and the outstanding qualities of my son Tim, and my daughters Lynda, and Ann? What wonderful adults they have become. As of 2021, Tim is 58 years old, Lynda is 56 years old, and Ann is 52 years old. I have many memories of them when they were children, teenagers and moving into adulthood, as well as all of them as adults. Keep in mind, as human beings, we are not perfect, and I was not a perfect parent. I did the best for them that I could. I always tried my best to put them first in consideration, wanting them to have the best life possible and enjoy life to the fullest.

Each of my children has unique qualities of greatness - and each one is totally different from the others. What shaped their lives? How did Gail and I influence their deci- sion-making, and what genes did they inherit from their grandparents and from Gail and me? Surely it is a mixture of many unique and wonderful qualities that each possesses, that they are giving to the church, society and to their children. Their gifts are remarkable.

Sometimes, when we give our gifts to others, it is difficult for us to see what it is that we are giving; but others see how superb our gifts to the next generation may be. Each one of us is making choices that change his or her situation for better or worse. We are not guaranteed a happy life, and life is a struggle of learning and adjusting to others and our situations. This goes on for a full life of growing, adjusting, maturing, and changing our minds about what we thought was right or wrong. Now, as my kids approach midlife, they see things differently than they did when they were teenagers or younger. We all have matured, learned and changed.

These are stories of their journeys, both good and bad, and what they have encountered as I watched their choices and their successes and failures. They always got up and started over again, so to speak. I am very proud of them and proud to be their father. They are generous and great in giving their gifts to others around them.

CHAPTER ONE: TIM

....

Medical Concerns. When my son Tim was born, he had club feet, and the doctors also told us his hips may be out of their sockets. This was too much for Gail to handle. She cried and cried. I was upset and didn't know how to handle it, but I had a sense that the doctors would guide us through this time and Tim would be okay. To our amazement and joy, we worked through these problems. First, the hips were okay; and the doctors put his feet in casts and then mandated his wearing a bar night and day to hold his feet together. They were able to turn his feet around. Tim, as a baby, could crawl, even walk, with this bar holding his feet together. He was later put into corrective shoes, to continue straightening his feet. We had no medical insurance, so we paid off the hospital and doctors with payments, slowly, over the years.

Did I have the right priorities? My main focuses in life were my work, the church, and the family. I now realize that this probably wasn't the best order. But that's somewhat because of how I was raised, and how many others of my generation were raised. A man's main concern was work and being a good provider. Women took care of the children; fathers provided the income. My main concern, to a fault, was being a provider for my young family. I depended a great deal on Gail to take care of our babies. We were very poor at that time, but I was happy as I could be with who I was. Depression had not become a part of my life at that time, but anxiety was certainly very high in my life. I worked numerous jobs during those years. And of course, the church was huge in our lives. In addition to work, I was taking care of a large garden, raising chickens, owning a dog, and volunteering at church. At the time I thought I was doing what was best for my family.

Mother love. Gail nurtured our children as they came along. Tim became more a part of my life as he grew older and entered the sports world that was open to boys. I wanted him to have no question that I loved him, so I would tell him over and over and over again, to the extreme, that I loved him and cared for him. I can remember him going to Gail and asking her, do you love me mom, because dad tells me that he loves me but you don't. Then naturally, Gail reassured him that she loved him very much also. So, I quit telling him over and over that I loved him in this extreme way.

When they were small children, Tim, Lynda, and Ann were there for Sunday school classes. It was wonderful that they got to attend preschool in church. I tried my best to show them I loved them and cared for them with words that

I would say to them. I was around them at night, and in the morning before going to work.

I was receiving counselling when the children were young, for anxiety disorder and fears and thoughts that I didn't want, and that I could not stop, but could manage through counseling. Gail accepted the fact that I was a good provider who needed counseling. She loved being a mother, and she loved our home. Gail was a natural at taking care of our children. What joy and happiness we had at that time in our lives, despite struggles with money, living in our first home, a small one-bedroom house on an acre of land, with good neighbors. Sometimes, in some ways, these challenging times are the best times in your life.

Great memories. Gail and I were so overwhelmed by the arrival of Tim, and pleased with what a handsome, outstanding son he was. Once we had his feet corrected, they didn't seem to bother him much during his march to adulthood. Tim was outstanding as a baseball player, and he graduated up through the years from T-ball to hardball. I can remember him playing T-ball in his sharp uniform and, of course, I thought he did great. When Tim was eleven, his team won their division championship and Tim was selected to the Portland all-star team. I can remember Tim playing football at Benson High School. You know, if we had been in a small town and not a large city like Portland, he would have been first string as a running halfback. He liked to play end on the line. He was a good catcher when the ball was passed to him by the quarterback. I was so proud that my son was carrying our family tradition of playing football. This goes back as far as I can remember, to my grandpa and then to my father, then to me, now to my son.

I can remember my dad coming to visit us and my dad and I building a racecar go-cart. That was a great time for us, and a great time of joy for my father. I don't know how much my children picked up on the pain and struggle we had when dad came to our house, but they'll have to forgive us. Why was this so painful? My dad would try to take over all decisions that we were making at that time. He was very intrusive and controlling and could not accept that I had become an adult. It was like he wanted to take over our checkbook; of course, he didn't, but that was how intrusive he was and demanding to know everything at that time in our lives. It was painful. But it was also a joy to have a father trying in his way, desperately trying, to help us, because he felt he knew best about everything. I hadn't yet forgiven him, that time in my life, and didn't understand him from a psychological point of view.

One of my best memories was when my parents were visiting me, and mom made a special trip to see one of the children, I can't remember which one, off to school for the first time, on their first day of school. I can still see them out in front of our house on Elliott Street. We took pictures of mom walking the children to school.

Tim's first day at school was like old hat. He did not cry or become scared or show any unusual emotion. When he got to his classroom, he hung up his coat, and went and played with the other kids, not looking back at Gail. I probably was off to work.

No learning disability. The other thing that I was overwhelmed by, and proud of, was that my son did not have a learning disability; he could write and spell, and he was also very good at math. These things that came so easily to him were, in my life, a nightmare for me. I was so happy that he was going to fit in with the other students and probably would excel at things he would choose. In my life, I couldn't join in on special activities such as writing for the school newspaper or working on the prom or going out for the spelling bee. I wanted to be a leader when I was in school, but I couldn't. Here was my son doing the things I couldn't do. I was so proud, and probably showed a great deal of exuberance towards him. I am also so very grateful that my learning disabilities were not passed on to Lynda or Ann.

A family pyramid. This brings me to something that is very important about our heritage, or seeing ourselves being helped by our parents and our grandparents and their parents. Picture a long line of individuals standing on top of the shoulders of one another. Tim, Lynda and Ann, standing on the shoulders of past generations – the heritage of both Chuck and Gail. These thoughts dominate my thinking about each generation giving something to the next generation that makes us unique and special, being able to flourish in some pursuit because of the family tree of greatness. Tim, Lynda and Ann flourished in school, but in their own individual ways. The Hanson tree (Gail's family) also contributed largely to who my children have become. My son Tim is very good at math, but he also has a hard time with remembering things that he has learned from the past in school. I'm sure he probably writes down things to remember when he goes to the store. Lynda has a good memory and is very precise in decision making. She makes up her mind very quickly. She is a planner and a plotter of thinking way ahead of other people. She knows exactly what her goals are and goes about making those choices to accomplish those goals. Ann was athletic and participated in dance and gymnastics. She was a neighborhood leader who always seemed to be surrounded by friends. We were always given a great report from Tim's schoolteachers about his progress and he was an exceptional student, always working with the teachers to further his education. Tim went to Benson High School where he studied to be an electrician, and in a way, followed in my footsteps to be a contractor. I think Tim could have had many options as far as his occupation. It seemed to us that he had a great many skills.

When Tim was around ten years old, I built a bedroom in our basement for him to have his own room. At that time, we only had two bedrooms on the main floor and this wasn't ideal for three kids to be in a small bedroom, one boy and two girls. This basement bedroom provided an ideal way for our son to have his own room.

An underground cave? What we didn't know was that Tim had started knocking a hole through the concrete foundation wall to make a tunnel to the front of the house - quite a distance. He had removed quite a lot of concrete and dirt and had made a large hole in the wall, like a small cave, before we discovered what he was doing. Tim had put some kind of barrier, such as a dresser, in front of the hole so it had been hidden from us. I think we went out of town overnight for some event, and Gail and I hired a babysitter to watch over our children. The babysitter discovered this hole, and saw the dirt. She told us about this. She told us not to tell Tim that she told on him. This, of course, was dangerous, and our son could have been killed if the cave had collapsed. Fortunately, we discovered this and put a stop to it. I don't think we were harsh with our son but showed restraint and understanding. Tim filled in the dirt and patched the large hole through the concrete foundation. He had been spreading the dirt in the back yard. Thank God we discovered this in time. I told Tim he had to buy the concrete and get it to the house. Gail took Tim to a store and purchased the concrete, went back to the house, filled up the hole, then patched the concrete wall. Gail and Tim worked together.

When Tim was a teenager, I had the great joy of being his basketball coach and playing on the same team in the church league. There were not enough adults for a complete team and we really needed substitutes. It was nice if you had ten players per team. In order to continue having Church of God basketball teams, the league allowed teenagers to play on the adult teams. In some ways, this was unfair to the teenagers because they couldn't play at the same level as the adults, so some of the teenagers sat the bench and watched the adults play. This was unfair, but life, in many ways, has unfairness. Tim and I spent many days and evenings practicing basketball and playing games. We had a basketball hoop in the alley behind our house. This was great fun for son and father.

Writing about Tim does cross over to family events where our daughters and Gail also were involved. I loved to camp and build campfires and set up tents. I really enjoyed those times we went camping.

A little scare. This is a story about Tim doing a very scary thing. On one of our camping trips, when Tim might have been ten years old or so, we pulled up to a campsite near a very small lake. It was getting late, with only an hour or hour-and-a-half of daylight left. Gail and I became busy with setting up the tent and building a campfire. Tim told us that he was going to walk around the small lake. We saw him take off walking toward the lake. Gail and I became a little scared and almost panicked, but I held my wits, thinking about what we needed to do. It was getting dark so Gail started swinging a flashlight so he could see us, and I started walking around the lake in the opposite direction to intercept our son, which I did. We found him, to our relief. He was okay and we were so relieved and happy. He said he was getting scared and very happy to see his Dad.

Another time, we went over to Eastern Oregon for a camping trip during Halloween week. I decided to drive my big truck that was like a bread truck. We loaded our tents and camping gear and off we went, I think to Prineville reservoir. I don't remember taking a boat. We took candy and had our own private Halloween party for the kids. We hid the candy among the trees, and the children had to find it. It was cold and there was snow on the ground. Gail and I and the kids slept in a tent. I snored so loud Tim tried to sneak out of the tent. But when he unzipped the tent, he woke me up and I told him to go back to bed. I went to sleep, and the snoring stopped. Hooray! It was very cold. It warmed up in the afternoons. I think we all had a great time.

Tim has gotten into rafting, and I have gone rafting with him, including a day trip on the Deschutes River, and many days on the Rogue River. On my own, about twenty years ago, I rafted the Colorado River with a hired guide service. I've gone hunting with Tim many times for deer and elk. On these trips I would harvest the animals, but Tim did not, except for on one trip, as he didn't like killing animals. He was very sensitive to this. This was when he was a teenager. One of the trips was over at the Snake River. I had hired a guide service with horses to take us by horseback to a drop Camp. This trip we were hunting for deer. The area was extremely steep and difficult to walk around. Because of the steep terrain it was exhausting walking around looking for deer. I had one opportunity that was impossible, where I came upon some bedded down deer above me, and I was looking into the sun.

Tim and Gail played around at camp, and also went on some hikes and were having a great time. However, they got onto a very steep bank they were climbing, and Tim knocked a boulder loose and yelled Mom! Gail moved over fast and the boulder just missed her, thank goodness.

After Tim graduated from high school, he went to Central Oregon Community College in Bend. He was also back and forth at different times coming back to live with us. He also attended Clark College in Vancouver, Washington and later graduated from Biola University with a Bachelor's degree in Business. In addition, Tim studied to become a paramedic. He worked as a paramedic for two years, working 24 hours on, then 48 hours off. I was building houses by that time. Tim would come over and we would pour our foundations and frame up the houses together on his days off. Tim's earlier job framing up houses for someone else was part of the training experience that enabled Tim to become a contractor later.

My dislike of unions. When Tim was living in California, he took a test which allowed him to become an electrician in a limited way, because California has a right-to-work law. Tim, in my mind, is very qualified to wire any house. He has the knowledge, and the way he was able to learn this was by wiring his own house and also his parents' house. He could do this legally in California without any restrictions. One of the things that I got mad about, and still do, is unfairness by unions in the State of Oregon. When Tim graduated from high school to become an electrician, the unions denied him this opportunity because they were filling their quotas of black people, women and minorities. And they didn't have room for him. In the State of Oregon, we do not have right-to-work laws. The State of Oregon is controlled by unions and wealthy politicians who make up rules that keep our state from prospering, where people have the right to learn and grow in whatever occupation. They want to keep the consumer paying a high price for services, especially in construction jobs.

Today Tim is a successful contractor building and remodeling houses and doing retail stores. He purchased a backhoe and bobcat so that he can dig and remove earth as well. Tim likes to build houses by doing almost everything himself – from the foundation to the roof, electrical plumbing, sheetrocking, installing doors, cabinets and floor surfaces. He is a one-man show. He also loves working on cars and is a self-taught mechanic. Tim has volunteered for the Deschutes County Search and Rescue which allowed him to be involved with searching for lost victims in the forest. Tim has done much volunteer church work. He was Director for six years at Camp White Branch Church of God. He has, however, experienced shunning for his liberal church views and now no longer goes to church, but still has many friends in the church.

Tim and his wife Deb have three children, Hannah, Ellie and Ben. As Tim grows older, he is slowing down, but he plans on building three homes, having another large shop, and remodeling a house he bought, and renting all four of them. At this time, he owns three lots to build on.

CHAPTER TWO: LYNDA

....

Independent Lynda. It is every parent's dream to have a daughter who wants to be independent of authority, wants to stand on her own two feet and make her own choices, for better or worse. I believe this is the goal of parents: to build a platform that is stable, so your child can develop into her own person, and be able to stand on her own two feet. A parent's job is to build the platform on which she can launch her life. From then on, children are free to do what they wish without parental interference. However, we care a great deal about our children, and always will. We will always have suggestions for them because we love them so much and believe in them. Lynda struggled with the middle child syndrome, and thus with her parents. We worked it out as we all grew older, and Lynda launched her life from the platform that we built for her.

Lynda was just a gorgeous, beautiful baby, with beautiful red hair: a lovely little girl. As she grew older, I can remember the boys chasing after her in grade school and she would kick them on the shins so they would leave her alone. She got outstanding grades and had no learning disabilities.

Lynda had many friends and brought them to our house. It was a safe haven for her and we enjoyed her friends. We also were like parents to a neighbor child named Stacey. She and Lynda were great friends and companions. Lynda took an interest in cooking and helped Gail in the kitchen. What great times we had.

Here are some things I know Lynda enjoyed. We taught her that it is a great thing to help people. We did this by having Guy Dean, an elderly man whom we called our adopted grandpa, in our home for special times such as Christmas. We also painted his house for free with volunteer church help. Lynda saw that we were involved in helping and teaching the Christian faith. I know she enjoyed the activities that the church provided for her and others.

Going out to breakfast. I made it a habit of taking each of my children out to breakfast so we could talk and have a quiet time between us. For me it was special. We would talk about whatever they wanted to talk about. This was one of the ways I tried to show my love, and how much I cared for them. Lynda was always planning ahead for our breakfast times together, and I know she enjoyed these times as much as I did. Her independent spirit of taking charge and becoming a leader with her forward-looking mind always stood out in her desires.

As a teenager, Lynda wanted to drop out of high school her senior year and go live with her brother Tim in Bend, Oregon, and go to college. She was also considering the Air

Force Academy for teenagers, but I asked her to stay in high school. As I look back, moving to Bend might not have been a bad idea, but I wanted her to experience the special years in high school. To my amazement, she did just that, stayed in high school. She continued being a cheerleader, and became student body president of her senior class. And she was elected a member of her high school Rose Festival Court. I was so proud.

Lynda learned to drive too SOON! Lynda wanted to get her driver's license so she could have the independence so many teenagers crave. I believe she was 15 years old when I taught her how to drive. These lessons were a special time, and I thoroughly enjoyed our relationship. She was a great student, a quick learner, and extremely focused on learning how to drive. I wanted her to not learn so fast, so this relationship with her that I enjoyed might last a little longer. It is a joy to have such a smart daughter.

Lynda's first marriage. Lynda's marriage had a huge impact upon our relationship. She was only 19, and I felt Lynda was too young to marry. I wanted her to go to college. I wanted her to not marry until she was older. However, I learned many lessons about letting go and letting your children do what they want to do because at nineteen they are looked upon by society as adults who make choices for themselves. That is the way it should be.

I liked Lynda's husband Stan. He was a fine gentleman with outstanding qualities. He was a special young man whom she wanted to marry. Lynda told me that she was getting married by a Justice of the Peace. We attended the wedding and had a reception in our home afterward.

Distance. Lynda's husband Stan was going off to the military and moving to Georgia, and Lynda naturally went to be with him. Gail would go and visit Lynda when children came along. I actually watched on, hoping and praying for the best for Lynda. Lynda came home with the children to stay with us during a scare when a stranger broke into her house while her husband was away. This was a traumatic experience for her, and we were there to help her. We were glad that she handled it so well. She was so strong emotionally with her head on straight.

Lynda and Stan travelled to Germany where he was stationed. They stayed for perhaps four years. They had four children: Steven, Kelly, Joe, and Emily. Their youngest, Emily, was born in Germany. Lynda and Stan and the children came to live with us for about four months after Stan's stay in Germany. Then, they moved to Grants Pass in southern Oregon. This was a small, remote city without many employment opportunities for them. This proved to be a huge problem. I do not know why or when their marriage started to come apart. They moved back to Portland, Oregon, a very good move for them. I wanted to help, so I suggested that I teach them how to build a house. We went forward with buying a lot and taking out the building permits. Stan did not want to do this. But Lynda did, so I taught Lynda how to build a house, and she received all the profits from building that house. Lynda and Stan got a divorce and Lynda went to school and became a dental assistant.

My next big involvement with Lynda was after the divorce. She was standing on her own two feet and didn't ask us for any help. She wanted to buy a house across the street from her house. She rented out her first house, financially a good step. The new house had a daylight basement with lots of potential. Because I was in the rental business, I helped her convert her basement into a small apartment that she could rent out. I rolled up my sleeves and went to work. It took over a month of hard work coordinating the electricians, plumbers, and myself doing the framing and carpenter work. I provided all the finances for Lynda as a loan to her. I showed her all the bills. A rental business is a long-term investment to get your money back, not a short-term financial investment. I was very grateful to Lynda, and also proud of her, for her return of our loan.

Bryon. In 1997, Lynda met and fell in love with Bryon. They wanted to marry. So, they sold their own houses and bought six acres with a huge two-story house, partially a log cabin, with plenty of room for their blended family of eight children. In many ways, this is extremely hard to pull off, trying to meet the needs of each child, changing the rules and wanting each child to accept this blending. Parents find themselves with no schooling to be parents. They stumble along, trying their best to give their children a good foundation, and it is up to them to build their own choices and find their own happiness.

Once their children grew up and moved away, Lynda and Bryon sold that house and bought a brand-new home that needed landscaping work, which Bryon did. They sold this property, likely for a profit, during the economic downturn.

Lynda and Bryon are hard workers, and entrepreneurs. They sold Christmas trees on leased land, and also started a business selling hanging flower baskets. They bought an old fire house and renovated it as their new living quarters. Then, Lynda had a vision of purchasing an old schoolhouse on a large lot, adjacent to their property, and turning it into an event center to host weddings, meetings or special events. They bought the land and school and worked slowly, adding first the parking lot, then storm drains, and a turning lane. They did this all on their own, with no bank loans. Gradually they began hosting outdoor weddings, and finally got a bank loan for more improvements. Lynda handled the government requirements and building inspectors. When the COVID pandemic came along, they were still able to host outdoor weddings. They did all this while working their full-time jobs, Bryon as an excavator, and Lynda working for Kaiser hospital.

Bryon is a wonderful man with charismatic qualities and talents as a contractor, and I admire him greatly. He was a wonderful choice for Lynda. I observed them and thought they did the best they could and maintained their love for each other. I believe Lynda and Bryon have moved mountains compared to most entrepreneurs. Lynda and a vision, and the guts to work at it and realize it. As of this printing, their event center is booked up for a whole year with events.

CHAPTER THREE: ANN

I am comfortable with my new baby. What a wonderful, beautiful daughter the Lord has given me in Ann. She was so tiny when I first saw her at the hospital. By this time, I had a little more confidence in myself. I could hold her in my arms, and no, I wasn't going to drop her, and I knew that she wasn't so fragile as I thought my other children were. We went on beach trips with the youth group, and took Ann when she was a tiny baby.

Before Ann was born, I was working as a hydraulic mechanic for Dupar Dynamics, working many hours and also volunteering for the church. When Ann was little, I would sometimes put her to bed at night and tell her I loved her, like I did with the other kids.

The fire on the second floor. It was about this time that we had a large fire in our house that burned off the back side of the apartment upstairs. I was at work and Gail called me, asking me to come quick: the house was on fire. I drove as fast as I could to get there safely. Gail had been out shopping and got home and put Ann in the back bedroom. Gail smelled smoke and went upstairs and discovered fire. She called the fire department, got Ann, and went over to a neighbor's house as the firemen put out the fire. Later, Gail put Ann back into her crib. Then, a large piece of plaster fell from the ceiling onto the foot of Ann's crib, just missing her. Thank God she was okay.

What can I remember of the things we did with Ann? We went family camping, fishing on the lakes. It seemed to me, again, that I depended on Gail to do one-on-one things with Ann. My involvement was with the total family. We also liked to entertain our friends, especially Don and Mary Swagerty, playing cards and doing things as a group. Ann, of course, would go to church with us every Sunday. You might say church provided young children with head start programs, getting them ready for school. I can remember Gail telling me about Ann, when she was around three years old, running through the house and stubbing her toe on something, and Gail said, "It hurt didn't it?" Ann looked at Gail and said, "I recognize it and appreciate it", and went on playing as if it didn't hurt much. This became a story about Ann that we told our friends over and over again.

Gymnastics. It is hard for parents trying to decide what is best for their children, sometimes having to give up our dreams of what we'd like our children to do. Gail and I wanted Ann to learn how to play the piano. So, we hired a teacher to teach her how to play the piano, and she hated it. I thought, as time went on, that she would learn to like it, but she did not. She begged and cried to take gymnastic training instead of piano lessons. Gail decided to take her out of piano lessons, still at a very young age, and start gymnastics. This was a great decision for Gail and Ann to make together. This also meant that, on her own, Ann would ride the city buses to her training sessions. The gymnastics paved the way to her future success on her high school dance team.

So proud of Ann's many talents. Ann organized having the neighborhood children come over to our house to help her bake chocolate chip cookies, oh so good! She loved animals, loved her kittens. We had a trampoline in the back yard. Ann spent many hours doing flips and enjoying playing with her friends on the trampoline. She loved gymnastics. Ann was on the dance team at Cleveland High School and became a co-captain of the team. She was so graceful and did the movements so well. As parents, we watched and experienced our little girl growing up and finding out how wonderful she was in her skills.

Teaching our children to ski on Mount Hood at Timberline Lodge was absolutely wonderful. Ann, being a gymnast and an outstanding athlete, took to skiing like she knew how to do it before we taught her. She was great. She always beat us to the chairlift. I remember that I was always the slow one and she was the fast one. Ann, showing how quickly she learned new things.

Ann was a great deal like I was in thinking and processing information. My father's demand of perfection somehow crept through me and my thinking that I must be perfect and that there was only one right answer. This was such a struggle for me and also a struggle for Ann.

Church's influence. Church was such a big part of our lives. We attended fundamental churches that can teach in a very harsh, brimstone and hell-fire way. We would always move to a liberal fundamentalist church when an evangelistic preacher took leadership of the churches we attended. This had a huge effect on Ann's life and the family. Tim was going to college and was living with us off and on. Lynda wanted desperately to move out of our house and away from my leadership.

At 19, Lynda married, and I opposed the marriage. In a teenage way, Lynda described me as a hypocrite, and not living up to the standards set by fundamentalist churches. I think for a while, maybe a year, Ann had this opinion about me too. Lynda was married now, and Ann was left all alone to deal with her father. When I walked into the room Ann would leave. It seemed for a long time that we could not talk to one another. She did not want to go to church, but I told her she had to go with us. During my breakfasts with Ann we talked, and slowly my relationship with her improved a great deal. I tried my best to reach out, to be supportive and helpful.

At this time, we joined a church that would help Ann through her teen years. We attended this new church for 14 years. It was another fundamentalist church. Our daughter Ann accepted Christianity as taught by this fundamentalist church. At some point, however, I left this church, not believing, anymore, in their doctrine.

How can one be a good parent? Can parents understand how teenagers interpret things? My disability, my depression and church teachings made understanding difficult for me. One of the great needs for teenagers is to cut the apron strings of their parents and become their own people. And their living at home with their parents during this time creates a natural struggle that all parents and teenagers go through. Teenage thinking can go on for years. Teenagers need love, forgiveness and understanding by parents during this struggle. If you are a strong-willed teenager, desperately wanting to leave the nest, you aren't going to understand a parent who is struggling with depression. With the church teaching that all human beings are evil, it is easy and natural for a teenager to call her parents evil and pull away. And Ann, having a sister who was four years older, was very likely to believe much of what her older sister told her. Then, future grandchildren can pick up on the vibes that something is wrong with Grandpa. What was I to do as this was playing out in my life? You forgive and let truths play out over the years. This was a very deep struggle for me, to understand that time did heal. There also was the Triangle Game that was being played out by myself, my wife and our children. It took me many years to finally figure out what the Triangle Game is.

Is It All Right to be Human?

When Ann graduated from high school, she chose a career as an occupational therapist. She went to college in Arizona for a semester and we helped her financially. She started saying thank you, dad for your help. She attended more schooling to get her license. Ann dated a man named Bryan for four years. They were married and had a beautiful wedding. One time Ann and her husband went camping and fishing in the state of Washington and borrowed our car, a jeep, and pulled a boat. On the way home from that trip, they got to Oregon in the middle of the night and the car engine caught fire. Ann was so distraught and apologized over and over. I said it is okay, it wasn't your fault. The car was on its last lap anyway.

Ann's marriage to Bryan lasted sixteen years. They had two very active and handsome boys – Preston and Jaden. Ann is a wonderful mother. She is very loving and expressive with her feelings to others. After her marriage failed, Ann came to live with us for about two years. She was devastated emotionally and financially pressed. We gave her space and let her healing process take place. We encouraged her to save her money. She was able to buy a house with an apartment in the detached garage in Vancouver. Her ex-husband died of a stroke and her children came to live with her full time. Now she is a landlord and has a beautiful home and yard. She is now also a grandmother and loving the experience.

A big family. We are blessed with a big family. Our three children had nine children of their own, and we have also welcomed four step-grandchildren into the family. We currently have twelve great-grandchildren. I do not know if I will live to see any great-great-grandchildren, but if I do, they will be loved.

CHAPTER FOUR: THE TRIANGLE GAME

··

I used harsh words to control my family. There was no excuse. I certainly was the prosecutor, trying to control everybody with harsh words, as my dad did. My wife showed nothing but unconditional love and support for me. Over the years, with counselors and my own desire to have a healthy life, I wanted to be the best father and husband that I could be. Discovering the truth always brings healing, though truth is often difficult to discover. In order for us to heal, I asked all my family members to quit playing the Triangle Game, and to love one another and support one another as we go forth with our lives. The truth shall set you free.

What is the Triangle Game? And how do parents and children play this game? This was one of the struggles that my wife and I had in our marriage and it took years for me to figure it out.

The Triangle Game is really a game of survival in some ways for one of the partners – it can be the husband; it can be the wife. First of all, husbands were often taught to be the head of the family and the wife was to be submissive.

Nothing is absolute, because a reversal of roles could be played in a marriage. One partner is obedient and does everything the other partner wants – because they think this shows unconditional love.

Gail and I brought this game into our marriage from day one. This is what Gail was taught by her mother, how her mother survived in a difficult marriage. Without question, my wife supported me and loved me and made the difference for my very survival as a human being. I could not have made it without her constant love and support. She is the greatest, the pearl that we all seek in order to find happiness. So often we meet someone who makes our lives so much better. My wife Gail gave her life to me. Without her, without question, I would have died, probably in my 30s or 40s, due to my depression. Gail also sacrificed as a great teacher to our children, teaching them what Christianity is all about. So many of my friends and family, and men I have encountered, have said to me that my wife made all the difference. They showed great envy, wishing they had someone in their lives so loving and supportive. Just think, she forgave me over and over again for my harsh words. I did the impossible, only because she was the wind beneath my wings, and we both soared to great heights.

The Triangle Game is played in many marriages and is a game played by father, mother and children, that can often be destructive in family relationships. In this game, individuals take sides. Some defend and try to rescue a member, usually one of the parents. The wife ignores the husband; over a period of years, she ignores what the husband is saying by having selective hearing. The husband also becomes the disciplinarian for the children, and the wife is quiet. Children do not learn how to make decisions or have a voice. And if the husband attacks or puts down the wife, which often happens, the children come to her rescue. I would use the word martyr. The wife is sugar and spice and everything nice and plays a martyr role. The husband is the prosecutor. Children defend the wife. In future generations, children often choose a husband like their father and the game starts over again. You have the prosecutor, you have the martyr and you have the rescuer.

I believe that my two daughters played this game of defending their mother, the martyr, and my relationship with my daughters struggled on into adulthood. My grandchildren also picked up on the vibes that I was evil, often from their church teachings. It took many years to work through this game. I simply asked my children, who are now adults, not to play this game. Slowly over the years, I have gained love and respect from my daughters and grandchildren. Hopefully, the game will be discovered and stopped. My pursuit of improvement brought victory to my family. I work on not being a prosecutor or attacking anyone in the family. I seek my wife's wisdom in decision-making now. We both struggle with decision-making. As you know, we don't have a crystal ball..

PART FIVE: OVERCOMING MENTAL HEALTH CHALLENGES - CHUCK'S KEYS TO SUCCESS

....

CHAPTER ONE: INTRODUCTION

··

As you have read by now, my OCD complicated my life and took up many, many hours of my days. And I felt powerless to stop the ruminating that made me feel helpless. Doctors aren't sure why some people have OCD. Stress, depression and anxiety can make symptoms worse. Sometimes OCD can be linked to physical differences in certain parts of the brain. As noted, there is no cure. Suggested treatments such as psychotherapy, relaxation, and medication never worked for me, and I have tried them all. I will try and explain what has worked for me in the next chapters.

My depression was at its worst when I was trying to learn Mindfulness. My OCD wouldn't let me stop after 15 minutes or so. When difficulties happened at my construction jobs, that could also send me to depression, occasionally severe. And I still experience it sometimes today. It is important to never give up and to keep searching for solutions.

From birth, I experienced Central Auditory Processing Disorder, which made it so hard for me to do well in school. Professionals suggest various coping strategies. These include having a work area which is free from noise and distractions, wearing ear plugs, taking advantage of tutoring, and learning to ask for help. I believe I have overcome many of the obstacles that CAPD presents. However, problems with hearing and understanding still remain with me today.

CAPD has severely impacted my life. How did I live with this problem and manage to work it out to live a successful life? When no one comes to your rescue to help you with this disorder, you have to seek your own solutions. Today, help is available to aid children, but that was not the case throughout much of my life. Dr. Davis, author of this book's Foreword, said that counselors did not know how to treat patients with this ailment. Each patient had to try and figure out what to do on his own. Then in around 2008, research started coming out with ways to help those with processing disorders cope. My recent counselors learned, to their amazement, that I was already doing most all of the things that counselors now tell their patients to do.

CHAPTER TWO: FINDING WAYS TO COPE

···

Experiencing occasional anxiety is a normal part of life. However, people with anxiety disorders frequently have intense, excessive and persistent worry and fear about everyday situations. Often, anxiety disorders involve repeated episodes of sudden feelings of intense anxiety and fear or terror that reach a peak within minutes (panic attacks).

These feelings of anxiety and panic interfere with daily activities, are difficult to control, are out of proportion to the actual danger and can last a long time. You may avoid places or situations to prevent these feelings. Symptoms may start during childhood or the teen years and continue into adulthood.

Examples of anxiety disorders include generalized anxiety disorder, social anxiety disorder (social phobia), specific phobias and separation anxiety disorder. You can have more than one anxiety disorder. Sometimes anxiety results from a medical condition that needs treatment.

Whatever form of anxiety you have, treatment can help.

- *Mayo Clinic*

I am now in my 80s. I have had to deal with OCD since I was in my 20s. You do not, at first, recognize that you are struggling with mental illness. It slowly creeps up on you. You don't want to accept it, but it is there, and you have to deal with it. There are so many pitfalls and dead-end decisions that can make it worse.

I started counseling in my 20s, at college, when l was studying to be a minister. I started receiving guidance about OCD from my counselor. This started a pattern for my life. I have had many therapists since then.

Some counselors and psychiatrists think OCD traces back to parents changing your diapers and dealing with your poop. Then the child must begin obsessing about going to the bathroom. So, it may start near the beginning of life. If this is true and your parents treated you severely in dealing with diaper changing or toilet training, it could have a strong effect on you for the rest of your life.

It was 1962. I got married and dropped out of college, but I was still seeing a counselor. I went to church, a fundamentalist church, which teaches that Jesus saved you from sin that you inherited from Adam and Eve and therefore you are evil. This teaching plagued me and hurt me for the rest of my life. Here I was basically trying to be a born-again Christian, but I was mentally ill. At this time, with my compulsiveness, I counted things such as how many tiles were on the ceiling.

I worked at various jobs over 40 hours a week in a deep struggle with depression and with obsessive-compulsive thoughts.

I desperately sought acceptance and wanted to be approved by members of my church. What the preacher said was absolutely true in my eyes, without question. This was, and may still be, a big part of my obsessiveness. I was in therapy for depression and anxiety disorder and also slowly examining how I was raised by my parents as I struggled with fundamental doctrines taught by the church. Behind it all, there was perfectionism. One must be perfect. How could I get rid of my evilness taught by the church?

How do you make good decisions when you are mentally ill and so stressed with anxiety and depression? You have to make choices, though they tell you not to make decisions when you are under duress. Am I evil? Should I ask preachers to pray over me to get rid of my carnal nature? Hollywood makes movies about such things.

My mental state became worse. Anxiety, depression and OCD were overtaking me. I desperately needed help. My teaching and training by the church and friends was that counselors are the sort of bad people that may lead you astray and destroy your faith in God.

My counselor knew that I needed to go to church. He guided me to go to another church in the same denomination. I learned that there are extremist churches and more liberal ones. One church did not have altar calls (where you go up to the altar and beg forgiveness for your sins) every

Sunday. I did well in this church. I felt loved, and accepted the doctrine of this church, as it was more liberal in how it was preached.

Forgiveness and no more counting. I knew of a college professor who had just retired who taught psychology at the college I attended. She also was a preacher within the same denomination that I attended. A part of her counseling was prayer, asking God to help me. I had a sense that God sent her to me, a sense that some great power is going to help me. The main thrust of the counseling of course was dealing with anxiety, depression, plus suicidal thoughts and OCD. She asked me not to count items in the room such as light fixtures or tiles. I stopped doing this. This became the focus of my recovery, which I worked on night and day. My depression greatly improved, and my anxiety became manageable. We also worked on forgiveness of my parents. This was accomplished by going back in time and learning about how my parents were raised and what their lives were like as children and teens. This brought forgiveness to my heart when I learned about my dad's early life. Now I could see him as a man dealing with huge problems. I also became grateful for the things my dad did give me. He did lay the foundation for me to be successful in business.

I have had at least six counselors in my life. So, what was it that helped me deal with my mental illness and helped me make some of my best decisions? Success meant my family was helped a great deal, that my marriage and my children reaped the benefits too. Did counselors ever make mistakes? Yes. But I hung in there with them and we made my life better because of it. Some church teachings I had started to reject, yet I tried my best to keep the faith. There was a God. I saw that the leaders and preachers of the church very definitely can be wrong. When you hang in there with a counselor, you begin to see that fundamentalist concepts are wrong, that educated people can help you and not hurt you, as the church implied.

I came to see that fundamentalists' beliefs that human beings have inborn evilness or carnal nature is totally wrong. How did I decide this? I noticed that this teaching from preachers and lay people in my church did not bring happiness or make life better; in fact, my depression, anxiety and OCD got worse. When I listened to my counselors it brought happiness, joy and success to my life. I believed there is a God, but on the interpretation of scripture the church taught – well, I needed to work through that. So, I changed churches many times. Wherever the preacher taught love and acceptance of one another and looked upon man made in the image of God, I got better. I stopped listening to preaching saying that we are born full of carnal nature. More liberal churches just did not preach it. This made my life so much better. What I learned from counselors and from reading self-help books in dealing with OCD gave me some healing. Here was the help I received to bring balance and mental health to my life and the strength to fight the battle, to talk back to mental illness.

Anger. Sometimes I would have very angry thoughts towards others, feeling my mentors were wrong, and my anger welled up in me. Those thoughts were not who I was or who I wanted to be. The fear of losing control overwhelmed me. Counselors said that I should not worry, I would never act on those angry thoughts, and they were right. The counselors suggested that I not struggle with bad thoughts, but only let them go and they will go away – and this is what I experienced. Thoughts of self-hatred do dissipate with time; but they are so deep within me. I wonder: will I ever love myself? At 81 years old, I still struggle. However, I enjoy helping others, especially teenagers and young people. I focus on getting them to learn to love who they are. Parents and church members have asked me to help their teenagers love themselves. If I had not gone through a painful life, I would not know the desperation that torments many human beings. It has become a focus of my teachings and mentoring of others.

The Bible teaches that if you think it, such as looking at a beautiful woman with desire, you have sinned. So, it teaches that your thinking can be evil. At times, preachers teach that if you are lukewarm in your Christianity, God will "spew you out of His mouth." This implies that you are separated from God, that you are devil-possessed or full of carnal nature.

I learned to choose more liberal churches because I hated myself so much and felt so guilty otherwise.

I chose counselors, and self-help books, because I found that this brought healing to my soul. How did I decide on taking the path of healing in my mental illness and not killing myself? I was able to give myself time to listen to my counselors and apply their teaching. I slowly got better. In time I could deal with the church teachings and figure it out. I told myself it is all right not to know the answers immediately.

Eventually I decided the Bible and the teachings of preachers and laypeople were wrong; that your thoughts and your thinking patterns are not evil. I even rejected what Jesus supposedly said, that looking at a pretty woman was lusting after her. Thinking is natural and God-given in both men and women, but things can go wrong with it. This was a huge breakthrough for me, that I could have my thoughts. They were not *plans,* merely thoughts, and harmless enough.

The brain as computer. But what was healthy about my thoughts? Your brain is a computer full of electrical impulses and chemical reactions; in other words, it is no different than the physical processes of your body, such as digestion. Each has a job to do and each can become damaged or not perform in the way it should. Thoughts are like the wind, they come and go, one does not have full control over them. There can be a deep fear that you will lose control of your actions because of your thoughts or impulses. People have thoughts rushing like the wind, but they can choose to dismiss these thoughts if they are bad or demand a bad action. There is no reason to fear losing control. Let them pass like the wind. It is not your fault that you have such thoughts, even those that your brain locks onto so you can almost think about nothing else. Do not resist or try in a desperate way not to have such thoughts. Think of a leaf from a tree that falls into a stream and gently floats away. If you do not resist your thoughts, they will slowly pass like the leaf or the wind does. You can tell yourself "that's just my OCD" and let it go. I learned that from one of my counselors.

It is a great relief to me to know that my obsessive-compulsiveness is not my fault. Slowly, over a period of a year or two, my anger gradually went away, like the wind. I slowly realized I was not guilty. I was not guilty for having a brain that was not working perfectly. Other people have similar problems at different levels of seriousness. Praise God, I was able to rise above my depression and OCD. Help came from many different places: counselors, movies, and kindness from individuals in the churches I attended. I was always very active in pursuing something that would help me. I did not give up on prayer and the concept that God was helping me.

Changing the channel. In the movie *The Aviator,* Howard Hughes taught me to change the channel to put something else in my brain. He did it by watching movies and comedians. Using those tools, he could think beyond his mental illness. So, television and movies became a great pastime for me. Also, the Burns book, *Feeling Good,* challenged me to incorporate his ten helpful concepts of how to process information. The first one on his list was "black and white, all or nothing" thinking. To me this once meant that I should become totally perfect as a Christian and that I had to be 100% perfect or God would reject me. I gave up this concept and worked on the idea that I didn't have to be perfect. One counselor asked me to start swearing. This actually felt so good! I didn't have to be perfect to be accepted by God. I slowly climbed out of my dilemma and eventually became successful in my business.

Just breathe. In the 1970s, I adopted a new exercise: I read what I spoke into a cassette tape, making my own tape to help me relax and breathe deeply. This helped me build my self-esteem. I listened to my tape at least once per day in the process of getting well. I still listen to it today. It still helps me to relax and feel good about myself. This was my first struggle between living or dying. Either I was going to climb out of my depression, or I was going to die. I achieved what had seemed impossible. I'd given myself time. I made the right choices. I started building my life in a positive way. How sweet this success was! To my joy, I didn't want to kill myself anymore.

Would I ever return to desperation and depression, and OCD? Yes, I would. But I knew that, through my learning as a patient, I could bring mental health into my life. Today I still see a counselor. I have tried to help others with the process of adjusting to a brain that doesn't quite work the way one would like. You can seek guidance from counselors, read books, and take up deep breathing. You can make your own tape in your own voice giving you sound messages.

Retiring. I was 58 years old and not ready to retire. I started to rebuild my life in a different way, making better decisions for the future. I sold some of my properties, but retained a duplex and a triplex, which I still own. At the age of 62, I took Social Security. The duplex which we lived in for 38 years was paid off. I did not really want to retire, but I was getting older and had some health problems. Finally, health issues forced me to retire.

Counselors told me one of the ways obsessive-compulsive thinking can overtake you is your concern with bowel movements. Those who suffer from OCD have thoughts such as these; as you look at people in their clothing and pants you visualize them having bowel movements. This does not go away. I turned to my health provider, and I again started counseling with them. Right away they put me on psychoactive medication. Drugs have always made me miserable, and they soon made me feel much worse.

Searching for the right prescription, they then encouraged me to take different medication, which had the same effect. I saw a therapist once a week for an hour each time. In some ways she was marvelous, and I worked through some problems. Then, I had the problem with her Mindfulness program, which put me in a terrible state where I ended up in the hospital for 10 days.

Yes, the ten days in the hospital in some ways was a good thing. But when I got out of the hospital, I was totally separated from friends, and deeply depressed. My challenge was to get off the drugs, so I started a withdrawal procedure. I am extremely fortunate that Gail was so supportive and loving and helped me during this time.

Good counselor, bad counselor. My HMO changed my therapist again, for reasons that I did not fully understand. My new counselor boasted that none of his patients need to counsel anymore. After a short period, he claimed, he could do the same with me. My interpretation was that his job was to get rid of me as soon as possible. After realizing this, I was disgusted, interpreting this as my reality. I quit that mental health department, and protested, telling them that this was not right and there was something terribly wrong at this program. I then sought a counselor outside of that program and found an older gentleman who was highly qualified. He also had experience with religion. I appreciated that he had his own personal experiences with churches and had a deep understanding of the history of Christianity. As I started counseling with him, he helped me with my obsessive-compulsive disorder and this obsession with bowel movements vanished. He also tried to convince me to look into drugs again, and sent me to a psychiatrist who came to the same conclusion as I, that there were no drugs likely to help me with depression. That brought me back to my own ways of dealing with depression, OCD, and guilt that has worked for me.

A bad idea. In the year 2016, I was shown a new, experimental treatment for depression. It was a daily treatment for 35 days. They put a machine on the side of my head and delivered a magnetic pulse to the brain. I was told that many people get better using this method. Being the person I am, I went through the procedure to get started on this treatment. I had two treatments. Each brought on terrible migraine headaches and I had to stop. I now had to be treated for migraine headaches. They are pretty awful. You get desperate for relief. It took me about a month to get over it. I am still experiencing some smaller headaches, but they do recede.

I will go on reading self-help books, seeing a therapist every two weeks and listening to my tape on deep breathing. I am letting go of thoughts. Letting them come and go; they disappear. Unwanted thoughts do go away and are replaced by good thoughts that I dwell on. I notice that physical activities release the endorphins in my brain and help me a great deal. Going to movies and watching a lot of television changes the channels of my brain, and I let the wind blow my thoughts away. This is how I've dealt with depression and obsessive-compulsive disorder. Whenever I can, I'm also trying to teach others in my church, as well as my grandchildren, how to deal with depression and obsessive-compulsive thoughts. I hope my three adult children will take advice from me now and then about religion and dealing with mental issues in their own lives and the lives of their children.

As a youngster, I developed an unusual talent for solving problems in all areas of my life. I listened and watched carefully, seeing what other people did when they were successful and what they did when they failed. Solving problems by watching what works and what doesn't work: it's sometimes called "horse sense."

Here are a few of my coping techniques:

1. Pretending to understand: Sometimes, when people speak to me, the message becomes scrambled in my brain. I don't get the message and I don't understand. When I was young and I asked someone to repeat the message, the response to me would be to treat me like I was stupid. If I responded with what I thought they said, that often convinced them that I was definitely stupid. Because of their reaction to me – friends, schoolteachers, and parents – I would act like I understood and got their message, and I would not return an answer if I could get by with it.

2. Quiet please: noise and confusion: I would hear everything, but really not hear anything. Sometimes I would tell people to repeat because of all the external noise going on. I learned that a quiet place was a better place to learn.

3. Sounding out words: Words can get all jumbled up. I solved this problem by finding other words to speak when I cannot sound out a word. A person's name is always difficult for me to say or remember.

4. Directions: Following a sequence or order is difficult. For years we had maps that would help us find an address.

As a contractor I had to find many addresses. I worked on this very hard. I still use maps even though there are now computers. My wife helps me a great deal in finding my way in the city. Computers have sequences that you have to follow in order to accomplish your goal. This is extremely hard for me to do.

5. **Rapid speech**: When someone talks fast or with a brogue or accent, this makes it almost impossible to me to understand. In my younger years I just pretended I understood. Again, I was often looked at like I was stupid. Today I confront the speaker if I have an opportunity to do so. I tell them they're talking too fast or that I cannot understand what they are saying.

6. **Give yourself time:** It is all right to be slow. I'm confused and I can't do what you're asking me. I don't know why, it just is. I will get there some day. Someday I will be able to understand. Someday. Just give me time please.

CHAPTER THREE: THIRTY-FOUR HELPFUL IDEAS FOR ME AND MAYBE FOR YOU

···

I have already talked about some of the coping techniques I have used over the years. Here are some additional examples. This is a comprehensive list of ways I have helped myself to handle many situations. Maybe they can help you, too.

1. Forgive your mentors. Forgive your mentors, they mean well. Mentors sometimes teach the wrong concepts, that you are at fault, and some churches teach that you are evil. Doctors, counselors and psychiatrists do harmful things to you, thinking they are helping you when, in fact, they are bringing you more suffering. Back in the 1950s, shock treatment was used and many patients were warehoused. Drugs have been prescribed that can make your depression worse and some patients do commit suicide. These medical providers meant well then, and they are still learning what might work and what does not. My parents did not know the mental health issues and learning disabilities I was facing. They did what they could, based on what they knew and how they were raised. Yes, they did a lot of very harmful things, especially my father – but I forgive them and thank them for the positive values they gave me.

2. Stay away from drugs and alcohol. I learned that drugs prescribed for my mental illness only made things worse. I believe one needs to try medications for mental illness to see if they help. A lot of the population receives some help from taking psychoactive drugs. I did not; in fact, they worsened my problems. And alcohol is never the solution.

3. Realize the brain is a physical organ. The brain is physical, flesh and blood, a chemical computer with electrical impulses that control your behavior. The brain is a physical organ that can be damaged. We know a schizophrenic person is born with mental illness, and it is not his or her fault. There are thousands upon thousands of people with mental disorders and their behavior reflects their inability to process information correctly. But should you call that behavior evil? The brain is complex, and we are still learning how it works.

4. Accept your processing disorder. Accept yourself and work on learning how to make good decisions. It is all right to not be perfect. It is all right to fail. It is all right to not be loved by everybody that crosses your path. I now understand that there is currently no cure for OCD and CAPD; you can only manage them. At this time, according to my counselors, I have put in place everything I know to manage my OCD that comes and goes. With good management, you too can live a useful, prosperous life.

5. Words to stop OCD brain lock. How can I stop the rumination? One can spend hours, days, ruminating and thinking about one subject. Stop it, yes, I said stop it! Tell yourself: "Self - stop it!" Or you can simply say "Oh, that's just my OCD" and drop it. Try it. There are books out there that can help with whatever mental disorder you have. I read and recommend for OCD the book *Brain Lock* by Jeffrey Schwartz. There are many books on depression; one I read is called *Transforming Anxiety*, by Doc Childre and Deborah Rozman, Ph.D.

6. Change the "channel" to new thoughts. Change the "brain channel" to a new subject or thought. Substitute some good thoughts. I use television or movies to refocus or change the channel. You might read a book. This helps a great deal to ignore the unwanted thoughts. Consider that the wind is blowing unwanted thoughts away. This will help you relax. The wind brings thoughts, and the wind carries thoughts away.

7. My three-word phrase. I began to use three words that help me with an automatic response to anxiety and depression. This creates an automatic pilot that your mind immediately thinks of to talk back to the thoughts that are negative. You must repeat these several times every day for 30 days to create your automatic response. My three words are "okay, fine, and handle." "You will be OKAY" are the first words that paramedics would say to calm your fears. They do not want you to go into shock from your injuries. The emotional anxiety needs to be challenged and calmed with the word "okay." Ninety-nine percent of everything I worry about and stay up all night ruminating about never happens. So "fine." "I am going to be FINE." In reality this is what happens. "Handle." "I can HANDLE whatever comes my way." I'm good enough. I'm smart enough. I can make good choices. I can handle this problem. These three words equip you in the battle to be won, in your struggle against anxiety and depression.

8. Write your story down. Write your story down on paper or use a computer. When you write your story, it is therapeutic, and it will help you bring forgiveness to yourself. Make an entry daily by writing a page or two. It is extremely helpful to bring forgiveness and understanding to yourself and to others. It is why I have written this book.

9. Develop humor in your life. I started collecting jokes and learned to tell jokes from memory. I have about ten jokes that I tell. This took time and effort. At the Senior Learning Center group I attend once a week, I get a chance to tell one joke at the end of the session. Others also have the opportunity, but often it is just me. Laughing with others helps in so many ways. Give it a try.

10. Other physical problems. At age forty I diagnosed myself as being dyslexic. This I believe to be true, because I certainly had all the symptoms of being dyslexic. I took a test at age 69 that revealed this learning disability. And I learned that it was not only a visual problem, but also a hearing problem. Wow, how did I do so well on my own? It's a miracle. Perhaps I used a great deal of my brain all the time. Who knows? Later, when I went into the hospital for open heart surgery, I was diagnosed with sleep apnea. I am grateful that the nurses discovered this. For so many years, I was so tired. I was tested and the clinic found that I was only getting one to two hours of sleep a night, even though I was in bed for six to eight hours. I got a respiration (breathing) machine, and now I sleep four to five hours a night. When my depression gets bad, I do take sleeping pills, but I try my best to keep that to a very minimum. My lack of restful sleep was certainly a result of my OCD, but other physical problems made it much worse. Continue to look for other causes.

11. **Use a light box.** I struggle with seasonal depression. I go through a struggle each year with summer turning into winter. I use a bright light box that you can easily buy, to bring the sunlight in the early morning hours when it is still dark with the night. I also walk outside, soaking up the sunlight at least thirty minutes every day. I consume doses of vitamin D and B12 that help with depression.

12. **Unconditional love from pets.** I have had a dog from childhood, and still have a dog today. Most of them have been hunting dogs. My love affair with dogs has helped me greatly with my emotional struggles. Pets can give unconditional love to you at any time.

13. Educated people in high positions are not perfect. I stopped assuming that ordained or well-educated people, even those with advanced degrees, are telling you the truth. I thought preachers in the fundamentalist churches I attended were always right in telling me I was evil and sinful. College professors, without question, were always right. Books, whatever the subject might be about, were telling the truth. But we are all human. No one has all the answers, no one is perfect.

14. Don't take everything literally. And everything is not black and white. I was taught things are black and white; there is no gray in life. A man must know everything and always be right. Girls and women could do no wrong, and I put them on a pedestal. This hurt me a great deal throughout my life, especially regarding religious beliefs. I had to free myself from this way of thinking. I no longer believe in the Bible as literal truth. I understand that many stories in the Bible are myths and told to explain the unexplainable. Fundamentalists teach you absolutes. I was always looking for absolutes. Finally, I began to notice they were continually changing the absolutes and the rules of human behavior. At one church I attended, dancing was a sin. Not many years later it became all right with that church for one to dance.

15. Search for the truth in religion. Ask for the truth and the truth will set you free. I believe most Christian churches teach that we have two natures. This comes from medieval teachings of Augustus regarding original sin and sex being evil. I now believe we are born in the image of God and we are good, not evil. This puts me in direct odds with many Christian churches. If God is speaking to us today, I believe he is saying that we all have grace and forgiveness. We are never separated from God. Many churches are still caught up in medieval times. The Bible was written by man, with the understanding of the science and knowledge present in their time.

16. Change churches if you must. If the church you are attending is not helping you and not meeting your emotional needs, making you feel guilt or shame for being a human being, change churches. Explore the foundation of their theology and the doctrine they are preaching and teaching on Sunday. In the last fundamentalist church I attended, there were three suicides in the church. I, personally, could not handle the guilt and shame their theology was preaching. It's a simple thing to leave the church. You just do it. There is a scripture in the Bible that talks about leaving a town or community that will not accept you. You shake off the very dust on your shoes and clothing and leave them behind. Most people tolerate the church's preaching because of friends they have within the church. They learn to ignore or not hear or face up to what is being taught. You must face up and challenge and leave that which is making you feel guilty.

17. I am not evil, and everything is not my fault. Teachers labeled me as stupid, telling me it was my fault. This made me feel guilty. I accepted this guilt, when I should not have.

I still sometimes feel that I am guilty and evil. For example, a friend of mine and I are walking down the street and he picks up a rock and throws it through a window. It is totally his doing, but somehow, some way, I will find a way to say I am the guilty one. I believe that God has unconditional love for every human, with no exceptions. I do have free choice. I am not guilty. It is not my fault.

18. Learn to love yourself. If I am going to live, can I love myself? Please tell me it's all right to love yourself. I developed my own way of finding goodness in me. Gardening gave me a feeling of accomplishment. I was the peacemaker with everyone, especially my parents. My dog gave me unconditional love. Successfully helping others continues to be so important. Be sure to improve your skills so that you can help others - your neighbor, your spouse, your children and your grandchildren, your friends, and your enemies. When others hurt you, you need to work toward the goal of forgiveness. Be assertive in seeking help. Accept yourself and learn how to make good decisions. It is all right to not be perfect. It is all right to fail. A plow horse goes slow and true and always makes it to the end of the field and turns around and does it again. I am a plow horse. I am of value.

19. Make friends. Always be making new friends. I personally like to cook, so for many years we had small groups of church friends come to our house for meals. I gravitated to people of humor who made me laugh. Friends can bring joy into your life.

20. Communicate with others who are questioning. You are not the only one who questions religious doctrine. You are not the only one searching for answers about how to handle OCD and depression. Listen to others, who like you, are trying their best to understand life.

21. Accept your shortcomings; work to improve. Do everything you can to improve yourself. Develop skills. Improve your ability to read, to listen and to speak. Walking is good. Exercise will release the endorphins in your brain and your depression will diminish. Doing this on a regular basis is important. See a counselor. I accepted that this was okay for me. It has evolved into many years of counseling. That's okay. Read self-help books, such as *Feeling Good*. In a way, my whole life has been, and is, about doing a service or helping others. With OCD, I am constantly thinking or ruminating about those in my life, my family members, my children, my wife, people in the church. How can I help them? Spending my OCD "ruminating hours" thinking about helping others always brings me a feeling of happiness: Make yourself happier by thinking about what others need and how you can help.

22. Talk to strangers. I love to talk to people one on one, especially strangers. I try to reach out and help. This is not for everyone to do, but I love being forward, bold and friendly in talking to others. It gives me purpose. Of course, when I fail, I feel a little bad for a while. What a great feeling when I have succeeded in trying to help someone! Many of the younger generation really want to hear from elders, and most would like advice. I worked up a packet of information on dealing with anxiety. I took a big risk in my church when I passed out this packet to a few people that I thought needed it. It wasn't always welcome, but at least I was trying. My packet is called *Unconditional Love*, which tells you that you do not have to be perfect. It is all right to make mistakes; it is okay to fail. You can rise from the learning experience.

23. Do what you enjoy. Your life's work earning a living is extremely important. You need to find something to do that you like. I was good at my work and it provided a decent income. Develop hobbies. Look for small things in life that can bring you pleasure. For me, hunting, fishing, game playing, downhill skiing, boating, eating out, listening to music, going to movies, watching television, trying to help others, hiking and playing sports, all helped. I joined a group called Learning Institute for Seniors. I go once a week to discuss current affairs and other things. I have the opportunity of presenting and talking about something that I am personally interested in. I get to talk for about 15-20 minutes. This is great fun rubbing shoulders with college professors, high school teachers, lawyers and doctors. I am no longer afraid of expanding my knowledge, when in my early years, rubbing shoulders with teachers was so painful. I still garden. I have a huge garden. Our home is on a half-acre. I have family over to help me eat the produce. I give away produce to neighbors and to church friends. We also host a big corn feed gathering every year when it is time to harvest the corn.

24. Check it out; ask questions. When I think something is terribly wrong and I'm being rejected or put down by someone or something, I talk to them. Use assertive communication with others to find out what's going on. You will find that 99% of the time, your thinking is negative, and that, in reality, nobody is against you; everybody has their own troubles. This can stop much of the bad thinking and rumination.

25. Read books to learn. Reading and learning from books can help rid you of shame and guilt. One of the first books I read challenged the concept that God was in charge of everything and responsible for everything and has a plan that you must carry out in your life. The book was called *When Bad Things Happen to Good People* by Rabbi Harold Kushner. The next book I read about the Bible was written by Bishop Jack Spong, *Saving the Bible from the Fundamentalists*. It deals with how the Bible was written and who wrote it. I next read *Jesus Before the Gospels*, by Bart Ehrman. These books will help you talk back to guilt and shame from a religious point of view that challenges the theology and doctrine taught in so many churches. I also read a few books written by a college professor who taught religious studies at Oregon State University. Marcus Borg wrote *The Heart of Christianity* and *Jesus*. These two books will help you with the possibility that there is a God and that the Bible, if understood, could be a book of faith. I am now reading on a college level. Since childhood, I have basically been self-taught. My wife has helped me with writing letters and with contracts for business. What a joy to be able to read. I'm like a kid in a candy store who has discovered the sweetness in the joy of reading. I now use *Dragon,* software which lets me talk to the computer, so that I don't have to type anything. *Dragon* has really helped me get my thoughts down on paper. The *Dragon* software isn't perfect and the output requires some editing, but it is allowing me to tell my story.

26. Be wise when seeking counseling. I have told of my problems with past counselors. Counseling can be a lifesaver. Finding the right counselor for you is very important. The movie *One Flew Over the Cuckoo's Nest*, starring Jack Nicholson, shows what can and does happen in mental institutions. Try to be wise about who you turn to for help with your emotional problems.

27. Don't share one's mental state with everyone. I shared my struggles with trained Christian psychologists for many years, hiding the truth from others, including my wife, my children, my church friends, and especially preachers. People may put labels on you, so you cannot share your disability or emotional problems if you want to be a leader in society or the church or be successfully employed. In other words, one cannot show weakness. In the 1970s, it was important to social acceptance to conceal that you had a mental disorder such as depression. I felt that people would not hire me to remodel their homes or build them a house if they knew. It was almost impossible for me to work closely with people at church, as they might eventually figure out that I was impaired. In today's climate it seems common knowledge that a large population struggles with some form of mental illness. It is not a big deal anymore to reveal that you are seeing a counselor. Just use common sense.

28. Have a good marriage; have the right mate. There are so many people I should give praise to. So many individuals have helped me along the way. But having a good marriage means so much. It is important to surround yourself with great support. We all need help and support. But it was my wife who supported me and loved me and held me at night when I was crying. Her support has been vital in my being able to lead a successful life.

29. Meditation exercises. I have about 10 different tapes that use sounds like ocean waves and other things to help me relax. There are apps on your phone or computer that offer this. Meditation is so important, and doing it on a daily basis will help you relax your brain with and refresh your mind.

30. Visual breathing. When you exhale, think of your breath taking all of your mind's hurt and guilt and blowing it out of your body. Just expel all the garbage as your breath leaves your body – sounds simple but it works, and it's wonderful.

31. Never give up. I have always been aggressive in seeking to improve myself. I learned that it is always great to utilize people around me who had knowledge that I did not have, and I was always willing to ask for help. You could say that I reached for the stars with an aggressive spirit. There were a few teachers and a principal who treated me as a human being with value. But most of the time I was trying to hide from the fact that I could not read and write. Still, there was something in me that always made me want to be a leader. I wanted to teach others – which often got me into trouble – but I didn't give up. My success in life has been my persistence. Cultivate hope.

32. Give thanks. Thank you. I thank God for all the people in my life who have been so helpful - the therapists I used, the friends I've made, college professors who were my friends. I am thankful for my children, who now as adults, are making huge contributions to other people's lives. I am grateful to those teenagers who have come back and thanked me for helping them with their spiritual journey. I still struggle with OCD and depression, but I give thanks to all of those who have made it possible for me to lead a successful life.

33. Give yourself time to process information. Labeling myself a plow horse for the farmer is of great value to me. I talk back to the negative attitude that things are my fault and I am guilty. If you are a person suffering from depression and OCD, there is a war going on inside that you must win with great courage. You may obsess about a subject that has no answer, ruminating about it every minute of every day. I use a few simple words to fight back the negativity and ruminating. Even a single word can help me fight and win the battle. My favorite two words to use now are "wait" and "be silent."

These come from the Bible: "I will wait on the Lord and be silent." This relieves me of my responsibility to search for an answer by thinking and thinking. I wait for the answer that God will provide me in the near future. He's not expecting me to find the answer by myself. So, when I start searching for the answer, I merely tell my brain to wait, and be silent. I trust the God of the universe to relieve me of unhealthy thinking habits. Then, calm comes over me and I can stop the obsessing and realize that I am of great value, and I'm not guilty. If you can find one or two words to use to talk back to the war inside you, you will find relief and calm. The war within will be won.

34. You're awesome! As I sit at my desk, struggling with depression, I see a small note given to me by a 13-year-old girl from a past Sunday school class I taught. It says, "You're awesome!" I look at it and pause. It helps me to think of my purpose in life, as a teacher, as a builder, and as a leader. This is part of my success, my accomplishments as a teacher. This young lady is now probably 19 or 20 years old. She has probably been thinking of college and appreciating those in her past, and how they have helped her. As I re-read her message, I believe it is true, that she recognized that I was a true believer and very open to who I was, and not a flake. I was there because I wanted to help improve her life, and I would like to think I did. If you don't have such a note from a former student, you can save Christmas and thank you cards and read them when depression comes.

CHAPTER FOUR: SPEAKING TO STRANGERS

....

I have already talked about how speaking to strangers helps me by giving me purpose and satisfaction - all important to better mental health. It is a challenge to know what to say to strangers and how to say it. People are cautious and have their armor on to protect them from a stranger. A number of years ago I decided that I would try my best to reach out and share a little of my life and try to give others something of value.

I have had many experiences: many good, a few not so pleasant. I wanted to make a difference in people's lives for the better, so I started experimenting with how to give comfort. I was also reading a lot of books on being daring and taking risks in life. Certainly, giving advice to strangers is not normal in our society and people may thank you, or leave your presence, or say "leave me alone." Most of the time, maybe up to ninety percent of the time, they thank me.

Most of my life I've tried hard to deal with my mental disorders. At the same time, I've been burdened by success: Why have I been successful, yet still suffered a great deal of pain?

211

Is It All Right to be Human?

What can I say to teenagers to help them? I often go on a four mile walk in Happy Valley Park which has a small wilderness marsh with lots of birds, some deer, some coyotes, rabbits and squirrels. A lot of people walk their dogs in this park. It also has three fenced in areas to run your dogs freely, and they play together most of the time. I meet all kinds of people I don't know in this park. I also discover that people from other cities come to run their dogs in the park and enjoy the wildlife. Surprisingly, most of these walkers are young women in their 20s and 30s; there are also men of various ages. There are young people, perhaps 13-year-olds, walking to school, and I wonder about their lives. You could say I observe a cross-section of America and what's going on with the heartbeat of the average American life as it struggles in pursuit of happiness.

What have I learned during my talks with these people I meet in the park? I have found widespread divorce, alcohol and drug addiction, depression, bipolar disorder, people struggling with family members, schizophrenia and other mental disorders. I have found a wide variety of religious beliefs that people share with me. What can I give these people that would be meaningful and maybe helpful to them?

My packet. In 2010, I worked up a packet of materials and books dealing with self-esteem, depression and where you can go for help for addiction and suicide problems. This is material that I have gathered over a period of years when handling my own emotional challenges. I give these packets

212

and books out, free of charge. I've given out more than 100 of these packets to people in this park and to their family members, when I think these books or information would make their lives better. Not a week goes by that I don't pass out this material to someone. Yes, it does cost money, but I buy these books and make copies of materials because I believe they can be helpful.

What do I say to those strangers to open the communication pathway, so they will accept my materials if they need it or if someone in their family needs it? I use Charlie Brown and Lucy's story and say I have some advice to give you and I won't charge a nickel like Lucy does. I begin by telling them I was born with the handicap of dyslexia and couldn't read or write well when I graduated from high school. I also share that I have used counselors over the years who have helped me deal with my life and have made it better.

This usually opens the door to their hearts, and in various ways I will then say, "How can I help you?" They may tell me about their deep struggles, with divorce, addiction, or depression. I then offer them my packet to read. I also may tell them I will pray for them. So many are in this struggle to make their lives better and do not know what to do.

A young girl with children. There have been a number of interesting conversations with strangers that went well for both me and the other person. For instance, a young girl with two children sitting by the duck pond. After I share a little of my life (my broken record), she then tells me about herself.

She is from Vietnam and has been accepted as a citizen by our country. She has a Master's degree in sociobiology and is currently not working, but raising her two children. She has a successful marriage and is doing well with her life. She volunteers to help disadvantaged children to read and write. Of course, this is one of my disabilities. I share with her how hard and shameful my life has been because of being dyslexic. This opens the door of mutual understanding. I thank her for helping others. She speaks four languages and looks so young to have accomplished so much. She tells me her father, during the Vietnam War, fought as a soldier against the Americans. How great is the USA for taking in this young woman, and how brave she was to come here and leave her family behind! This conversation goes on for over an hour and as she has to leave, I offer her my packet, but I do not have it with me; it is in my car. She wants the packet, but she doesn't want to go there with me, if that's all right. Later I meet her on walks. She comes and greets me with a big smile. I meet her husband, and we are certainly friends. She made my life so much better by just talking to me. After this experience I started carrying materials to give out in my backpack so those who wanted it could have it right away. This relieves people of having to trust me to go to my car. I recognized this was a potential problem and learned from it.

Rewarding hugs. My walks in the Happy Valley Park have been "happenings," which brought joy and happiness to me and many with whom I've talked. I've met other people who became my friends, who greet me with a big hug when we meet each other. There is a lonely older lady, in her 80s; we talk sometimes for an hour and she gives me hugs. Sharing our lives is wonderful for her and me. I talked with a middle-aged woman with teenagers and gave advice to her about her teenage daughters and her husband. She was a flower child in the 60s or 70s, on drugs. She became pregnant, the man left her, and her parents disowned her when she was barely a teenager. Somehow, she was able to rebuild her life and found a husband and has additional children with him. She told me about a friend who was in bed with depression. On my first encounter with her she trusted me, and we went to my car and I gave her the packet. The next time I saw her she came running up, grabbed me, gave me a big hug and thanked me for the materials. She said she had also used counselors to rebuild her life. She came to me and talked up a storm and I listened and shared whatever I could to make her life better – it's about her teenage daughters and her struggles with them. One time I was walking my dog and she was driving her car. I looked over, she pulled over to the curb and stopped and got out and ran over to me and gave me a big hug and we talked for a while. These are successes I've had; but there have also been failures. Sometimes I suffer a great deal over those rejections.

A feather tattoo. Once I went into my pharmacy and was waiting, looking for a chair to sit in, and I saw a young girl – maybe 19 years old – with an unusual tattoo on her neck, a feather. I sat down beside her and asked her about the feather on her neck. She said she was honoring her sister who had recently died. I said I was sorry, and I asked her about her prescriptions that she was waiting for and why she was there. She said she had lupus and her kidneys were failing. Oh my God, what do you say to someone so young and facing death? She got up and got her prescription and came back and sat next to me. I told her I have major heart disease, which I do, and I'm waiting on prescriptions for my heart and other ailments. I told her I am so sorry that she faces these things and that I am a believer in God, and I will pray for her and I care a great deal about her life. So, we had a prayer. I got up to get my prescription and came back to her and reached out to her by putting my hand on her shoulder and saying I will continue to pray for you. Then we left together and went our separate ways. Oh, how she touched my heart. I wished I could give her a long life, but I can't.

Losing a wife. I like to fix things, like old things, by restoring them. I bought an old fiberglass boat and started the process of rebuilding and restoring this old boat. I needed advice and I needed some materials to rebuild the boat. I had to go to Tigard, Oregon to pick them up. I met the owner of the business and I started talking to him in a personal way. He told me what he was facing in his life. He was about 50 years old and he told me his wife was terminally ill with cancer and didn't have long to live. I did not know what to say except "I'm sorry and I will pray with you, and for you." He wanted to talk about his wife dying. So, we sat down together, and he poured out his heart to me. I listened and shared that there is a God. I listened to him for over an hour, and I went away so blessed by his positive way of thinking and by how strong he was. It's natural that I would compare my life to his and wonder how I would deal with losing my wife. Thank God that's not happening to me right now.

Football. In the fall I go to football games at the University of Oregon. I have season tickets and I talk to the people around me and learn about their lives in a deeper way than most. I watch the beautiful, middle-aged lady in front of me, and her husband or partner, as they watch the game with us. The lady on my left works in a hospital dealing with suicidal and addiction patients. She divorced, and remarried about a year ago. Back to the lady in front of me: She comes drunk or feeling good to all the games, and she is all over her husband in a sexual, honeymoon way. I waited three seasons of football before I offered her my packet. She also is a nurse working in surgery for heart patients. I think she is probably an alcoholic or a weekend binge drinker. She received my packet, thanking me; however at the next game, the couple seemed mad and would not talk to me normally, as in the past. At the next game, the nurse on my left, to whom I also gave a packet, thanked me and told me she made copies of the material and passed them out to her patients, doctors and fellow nurses. Naturally this made me feel good. But as for the other nurse, I suffer emotionally over her rejection of me.

I can only hope that she will consider getting help for her alcohol problem.

The boys. Several years ago, as I was walking my dog, I encountered six 13-year-olds walking to school. I have a routine where I step off the path or walkway and bow like Asians do when they greet one another; I remove my hat and verbally wish them well and have a great day at school. These young boys were very curious about me. I told them about my life as a 13-year-old, that I had a learning disability, and was treated badly by parents and teachers. In essence, that I was ashamed of myself and did not like myself. What can I say? What is it like to be a 13-year-old dealing with life? I told them that the foundation for success was to learn to love themselves.

As the year progresses, they keep stopping by to ask me to give them advice. I ask them to give themselves hugs by wrapping their arms around themselves and they do it. As the year goes on, I advise them not to compare themselves with others but to accept that they are different from one another, with different skills, different talents, and this is fantastically great! It's all right to be different.

Sad to say, one of their classmates, at age 13, committed suicide. There is so much suicide in our society. The school was in total disarray and emotionally very upset. I tried my best to calm the boys down by teaching them my three words that "it's okay," "everything's going to be fine" and that "I can handle it." The word "okay" is code for them to realize that their lives will work out okay. I said nothing else, but as they stood before me, they threw their arms around their own chests and gave themselves a big hug.

How wonderful to me that they had listened and believed that my ideas could work.

I have about five or ten minutes as they walk to school to give them advice about their lives and how to be successful. Love themselves, help others, gather information, show love and appreciation to parents and schoolteachers: Respect girls. Don't drink alcohol. Don't use drugs. Abstain from sex until you can pay the bills and be responsible for raising a child. I've tried to stay away from politics and religion. The group has expanded to sometimes include eight young men, and sometimes girls. Our society makes it very difficult to be a neighbor and reach out to others. I would like to think of myself as a sort of Mr. Rogers, conveying love and being helpful to my village before I die.

I'm aware I'm basically a stranger and that their parents may become afraid that their children are talking to a stranger. So, I write out my three words on a paper, telling them to look at the three words every day for 30 days. I also put my name and phone number for a parent to call me on the phone. I received two phone calls from parents. I wanted to calm the fears of the parents about who is talking to their teenagers on the way to school. Later, our relationship expanded to include their parents. I was invited to a birthday party for one of the boys. At times, a parent would come to my house to visit and talk. At the end of the school year, I had a barbecue at my house for the boys and parents. I set up a ping-pong table for the boys to play and also a game called croquet where all the six boys could play and be involved - they loved it. Once the COVID-19 pandemic flared in early 2020, I did not have a chance to meet with any of the boys in person for a long time. I missed this connection.

A note about teen suicide and addiction: I believe that adults need to step up to the plate and tell young people that they have value, that they are loved. If we tell them the truth, that the world has a place for them, I think there would be so much less teen suicide, addiction, and pain.

Twenty-dollar bills. I give away money to be helpful to the needy; usually it's a $20 bill. One time, I was in a grocery line buying groceries and in front of me were people who could not totally pay for their groceries. I stepped up and paid the difference. I gave $20 to a friend who cooks once a month at a shelter program. He cooks over half of the food at an Episcopal Church in downtown Portland. Quite often, I will buy someone a meal in a restaurant. Sometimes street people who are hungry come in out of the cold, and I will offer to buy them a meal. Usually, they accept. I've helped people begging for money at street corners and in front of cinemas in downtown Portland. I go up and talk with them and try to find out about their lives and why they are begging for money; they are usually young teenagers who melt my heart. I will give them $20.

Recently, I came upon a well-dressed man begging for money. He was attired for the cold and rain. It was very cold out. He was 71 years old, trying to live on Social Security, renting a one-bedroom apartment, and could not afford to buy food. So, he paid the rent and begged for food money. I gave him $20 and advised him to move to another state where it was cheaper to live than in Oregon. That is sad, but it is also true. How do I know? I live here.

Addiction. A young man was sitting on a park bench as I was walking in Happy Valley Park. I noticed him because usually nobody sits on that park bench. As I walked closer to him, I could see his face; he was crying. I wondered why. He was probably 18 or 20 years old, a very nice-looking young man. Other people were walking by and not taking notice of him. I went over and sat down next to him and start questioning him about his life and what was going on. He just said he was upset about something and he's not a talker. I tried to convey to him that I cared about him and that others cared about him. Because he wouldn't talk, I started talking about my personal life, and my struggles with life. My usual story is that I'm dyslexic and was mistreated by parents and schoolteachers. I tell people I struggle with depression and have learned how to manage it. The young man stopped crying and acted as if he wanted to hear more about my life. He asked, "can I talk about drug addiction?" I told him that I chose to not drink or take drugs as they only make things worse, and that I sought counseling instead of painkillers to medicate myself to handle problems. I told him about my packet of information and books that I give out. I asked him if he would like to take the packet and he said yes. I told him that it was in my car, a little way away. We walked to my car and I gave him my packet and books. I also gave him my telephone number in case he ever needed someone to talk to. We parted company. This is a short version of what took place; we were together maybe an hour. A week went by. He called me and said that he was in a good place mentally and thanked me for the material that I gave him. He never called me back again, but maybe I helped him. What did he do for me? I realized I had no information about who to call for drug addiction or alcohol addiction or suicide prevention. So, I gathered this information and now include it in my packet so that people would know who to call if they need this help.

According to the Centers for Disease Control and Prevention, suicide was the 10th leading cause of death in the United States in 2018, and second leading cause of death among individuals between the ages of 10 and 34, outpaced in this group only by unintentional injuries. It became important to me to include information about how to stop from committing suicide in my packets, to give people a way to find help. There is always a way out, if you know where to look. I think if our society just practiced the Ten Commandments, perhaps our young people would stop committing suicide.

Two ladies. I walk into a restaurant, IHOP on 82nd Avenue, close to Foster Blvd. in Portland, Oregon. I meet a friend of mine every Wednesday for breakfast. As I'm walking to a table, I see two ladies next to my table and I start talking to them before I sit down, and they want to talk. In a few hours they are going to catch a plane to California and leave Oregon. Their faces look like they are in pain about something. The conversation goes on about life and they tell me their parents are struggling with their emotions and perhaps depression. I open up and tell them that I suffer with depression and found that counseling with a trained counselor is extremely helpful. I am out of my packets and books, so I tell them my three words and how they have helped me deal with my problems: "it's okay" and "everything's going to be fine" and "I can handle it."

A struggle with different thinking. I've had many good experiences, making new friends as I walk through the park. There is always going to be someone who disagrees with you, though. As Brené Brown said, there's always someone to "kick you in the ass and you find yourself laying in the arena of life face down in the mud." In my case, this was a group of Jehovah's witnesses. They brought fear to my life with their unfriendly stares and even sometimes their words. It seemed to me they were filled with hate. I wished they would come and sit and talk with me, but they never did. I became concerned for my safety and started carrying pepper spray with me on my walks. So far, I have not had to use it. Of course, they do not understand me or my motives in making friends.

223

The COVID virus robbed me of the joy of making new friends. My purpose in life was temporarily shut down. Perhaps someday I will be able to work with schools or churches in sharing my packets, particularly with students.

A purpose for living. In my 70s, I met a young man who was in a halfway house. After doing a stint in prison, he was being helped to gain a foothold in society. I offered this young man employment. I provided transportation for him, picking him up at the halfway house, bringing him to our house to work for us. Gail and I cooked lunch for him; we gave this freely. I earned his trust, and we had long conversations about life, and I listened to him and tried to give him counsel. He chose to break the rules of the halfway house, and things weren't going well at our house either. Sadly, I had to break off the relationship.

Another time, I came upon a man living in the back of his truck with his wife. I talked with him about helping us with our yard and garden. He was delighted to come and work for us. We cooked lunch for him, and at times provided transportation to and from various locations. I believe he helped us for four years, and we helped him out in return. During this time, his wife died, and we tried to provide comfort to him as best we could. We encouraged him and even looked for full-time employment for him. He eventually got a full-time job driving and delivering packages. He found a place to rent, and he was in a much better place than he had been when we met him. This employment lasted about two years, until, for reasons unknown, he was fired. He became homeless again, living once again in his truck. He came to work for us again. Sadly, he had a major stroke and was hospitalized. Gail and I visited him at the hospital and tried to give him encouragement. However, he was now on disability and could no longer work. Once again living in his truck, he called me several times for help. I responded as best I could. Over the next few years, we lost track of him. Perhaps survival of the ups and downs of life is one of the key elements to having a purpose for living.

Mother taught me to help others. That is a good purpose, and it also makes you feel good. So, if you are reading this, go help someone. It will be good for your soul.

I could go on with many stories of acceptance and occasional rejection in my endeavors to talk to strangers. It is a learning experience to use the right words to make people's lives better. I have decided to continue talking to the six boys and to meet their parents occasionally. Talking to others is an important part of my life.

PART SIX: MY SPIRITUAL JOURNEY

....

CHAPTER ONE: INTRODUCTION

....

I believe there is a universal power for guidance and wisdom that is passed on to human beings. We call it God.

Is it all right to be a human being? My spiritual journey has been a quest, trying to figure this out. I assume there is a God. I assume that if we behave in a certain way we will be accepted by God and live forever in heaven with Jesus Christ. In my spiritual journey this means conditions and performance and behavior will determine whether I get to heaven. Most churches and belief systems revolve around this concept.

Religion has been a big part of my "Life Story." If you have read the first part of this book, you know I've already said a lot about religion. My fundamentalist background caused me much emotional trauma. Shame and guilt were at the core of my problem. My disabilities contributed to my lack of self-esteem. My wife and I changed churches many times. I began moving away from more fundamentalist teachings to more liberal interpretations. I was questioning and searching. I am now not certain that going to church is always beneficial for me. But I do believe that, from our birth to our death, God accepts us and we are all bound for heaven. We are not separated from God. We are judged fairly with mercy and accepted as we are.

CHAPTER TWO: MY JOURNEY FROM ONE CHURCH TO ANOTHER

•••

Christian Fundamentalists believe that the Bible is the inspired Word of God and that within its pages lies the Hope of all the world. They believe that Adam was the first person on the face of the earth and his wife. Eve, was made a help mate for him. They believe that Adam and Eve were deceived by the devil or the serpent and were driven from the presence of God. Because of Adam's transgression, God placed a curse on the human race. Since that day all men are born sinners by nature. Because of his carnal nature, Man began to obey that nature and do things that were against the nature of God and God became displeased. They believe we must repent of the sins that we have committed against him; fall on our face and be sorry for them; ask him to forgive us, having faith that he will forgive. This we call forgiveness of sins which is the first work of grace.

When this is accomplished, Man must then begin to seek the saving power of His grace, which is Sanctification by the Holy Ghost. This is the second work of grace. Without Sanctification no person can be saved. Without the sanctifying power we will, by nature, start

back to sinning; so it is absolutely necessary to have these works of grace in order that we may be placed back into the Grace of God.
- *Monta Vista Church of Christ*

I was born into a country that experiences Christianity in many forms. What were the seeds that were planted in my heart, in my soul, to the very core of my being? My parents were not religious, just attending church on special occasions. They sent me to summer Bible teachings, and I did meet outstanding adults who showed a great deal of love for me. I don't remember criticism or being put down by them.

My Grandmother was from the old school, raising her children in the Methodist church. She had been taught that you must be saved to be a Christian. As her grandson, I saw her as a tower of faith. She believed in God and she would pray. She seemed to me, most of the time, at peace with herself. She was a quiet person, not saying much, just living the good life. I can remember my grandmother, when I was a teenager, telling me the Christian faith was extremely hard to live. I was not sure how to interpret this. She buried three husbands in her senior years. As adults, her children attended different churches. It seemed to me that my parents did not have a strong belief in Christ. It was one of those things we didn't talk about. Deep down inside me, it seemed that my grandmother's Christianity had given her peace and happiness. It seemed that our friends who attended the Presbyterian Church also had peace and happiness. Through becoming a Christian, or accepting Christianity as the foundation for my life, I thought that I too, would have happiness and peace.

The Church of God. While I was in high school, this church taught me that I was evil, and that what my parents taught me missed the mark. You had the core of evilness, called carnal nature, which you inherited from Adam and Eve. I was told that I'm worthless and evil and need to be saved. I can remember standing in the pew of the church, as they were singing "Just as I Am," saying to myself, if I come to the altar, God will save me. I felt so terrible inside myself. The church was saying to me that I must be perfect. I felt that I was worthless. My parents are evil, and now my friends are evil because they are not saved, and I am separated from God. I felt very confused and very guilty.

Finally, I got saved, and the church members rallied around me, giving me hugs and praises. I had finally found a group who gave me praise and who accepted me. I kept attending this church. In my mind, I felt that God had guided me there. But no matter how many times I begged God to forgive me, I couldn't escape the fact that I was evil. But I couldn't really understand this either, so I put it in neutral saying that I would understand it in the future. I would work, I would study, I would read the Bible, and I would gain understanding. The church, it seemed to me, was using me as a trophy, and the preacher was showing me off as "saved." I left my friends, just making friends within that church. I suffered greatly with guilt and shame inside. I actually could feel the chemistry in my brain going from happiness to depression. But I couldn't leave this church. Later I would learn what cults do to individuals like me. Cults start dominating your life.

Warner Pacific College. Many of the students there attended a fundamentalist church – the Woodstock Church of God. Again, the preacher was hell and brimstone – you must be saved. I was almost at the breaking point of a nervous breakdown. My anxiety level was extremely high, and my feeling of worthlessness was there.

My goal was to eventually become a preacher. While at Woodstock Church I had an opportunity to preach, which I did in a very emotional evening service. It went well. Of course, I said words that everybody wanted to hear – I had learned the Christian words, and the Christian language of what a fundamentalist would say to be accepted.

A counselor helped me decide that I shouldn't be a minister. This counseling would change my life and head me in the right direction. I was now three thousand miles away from my father's dominance. I had to stand on my own two feet and make my own way.

Richmond Church of God. After Gail and I got married, we were both encouraged to participate in this church. Pastor Ely and his wife were very loving and supportive of others and didn't preach guilt. Unfortunately, after Rev. Ely moved away, the next pastor was an army chaplain. He ended up being a disaster for our church. While he didn't preach guilt, he was very dogmatic, in some ways like a dictator. Over the next two years church attendance shrank dramatically. We had many disagreements with the pastor, so we, like so many others, needed to move on to a different church. Gail and I discovered that many of the fundamentalist churches preached different Christian messages – surprisingly different from one another.

Holladay Park Church of God. While I missed being in a leadership role here, we did participate in the life of the church. It seemed to be a good fit for our children. Then the preacher resigned, and the new preacher took the attitude that most members of this congregation were either not Christian or had backslid. I could not stand this and thus, again, was faced with selecting a new congregation.

Tigard Church of God. Our children enjoyed a good youth counselor during our time at this church. I had come out of a deep depression and was doing well with my life. However, this was the time my counselor called my pastor to tell him about my emotional problems. This meant I would have constant conflict with this pastor. I believed my children were being helped a great deal by this church. I felt that God had guided me to this church, and I didn't want to leave. However, it was at this church where I ran into problems with the homeless shelter project. The leaders didn't believe my concerns, and I lost my standing as a leader.

This was also the church where I had differences with the church leaders about a mission trip to Costa Rica to help build a new church there.

Eventually, a new preacher was chosen, another hellfire and brimstone pastor; close to half the congregation left.

The United Church of Christ. This church bragged that "Whoever you are, wherever you are on your spiritual journey, you're welcome here." For four years I was welcomed and felt good about attending this church. But then we got a new preacher, who was an outspoken Democrat. Why was a preacher teaching from the pulpit theology using a political bias? I am an outspoken Republican who supports conservatism and our Constitution. At that time in my life, I was reading books by Marcus Borg, a teacher of religion at Oregon State University. I read a couple of his books on meeting Jesus for the first time. I wanted to discuss this at the weekly breakfast club bible study group taught by a couple who were ordained Baptist ministers and avid Democrats, as well as members of the church. Just wanting to discuss the topic of whether Jesus was really born of a virgin made some, not all, too uncomfortable. These leaders were against the teachings of Borg.

So, one of the leaders took me to lunch and basically took me to the "woodshed." He said I should be put in jail for just talking about these ideas. The Communists put people in jail for sharing opinions that differ! So, I had no choice but to stop going to that bible study group. That person suffered no consequences from the church leaders for what he said to me.

As months passed, I expressed my support for the free enterprise system to the new pastor. She did not support the free enterprise system or support the Republican party. Her sermons were supportive only of the Democratic Party. She rejected me for being a Republican. Both the Baptists and our new pastor were saying to all Republicans, "You're not welcome." It seemed that to be accepted you must be aligned with their politics. The congregation prided itself on being open and accepting – but was it really? So, again, I had no choice but to leave this congregation.

The sadness of leaving a church. I had gone to many different churches to find out what they teach, and to learn about their doctrine. I had been going for 38 years to fundamentalist churches, and I could no longer support them. I realized it is all right to grow spiritually and seek out a group that you can support. This means you will go through a grieving process that is like losing your spouse or your best friend. As I got up the courage to leave this last group, some of my close friends would not be my friends anymore. Many friendships changed. We still appreciated each other, but we just had different doctrinal views now. I left judgmental concepts, harsh God concepts. I left a church that rejected people and called them evil. I became liberal, more open to others, and to different ideas. I had been confined to a box of thinking, rules and regulations to be accepted. I left, but I began building new friends and constantly trying to learn new ideas that God had for me.

CHAPTER THREE: THE BIBLE AND ME

....

Where does biblical literalism come from? What is the genesis, if you will, of the habit of mind that makes many Christians read the Bible with a different brain to the one they'd use with any other writing? It is by no means an essential Christian tenet. No creed says anything about how to read the scriptures. The highest claim the Bible makes for itself is when the writer of Paul's letter to Timothy says the Hebrew scriptures were "God-breathed", which is wonderfully suggestive but hardly precise or dogmatic. I mean, Adam was God-breathed, and look what happened to him.

The Bible is the word of God, Christians believe, but why should the fact it's God's mean it has to be read with naive absolutism? Part of the problem is historical. The deification of the Bible is a result of the Protestant reformation. Before then, the final authority, the ultimate arbiter and source of information in religious matters was the Church, with its ancient traditions and living experts. When Martin Luther and friends opposed the teaching of the Catholic hierarchy, they needed a superior authority to appeal to, which was provided by the Bible.

- *Steven Tomkins, The Guardian*

I had begun to realize that in the United States there are many interpretations of the Bible. Many leaders rose up and established different churches, often proclaiming they had the absolute truth and could correctly interpret scriptures. I began to move away from the more literal fundamentalist interpretations.

The Bible as the literal holy word. I was taught that the Bible was the holy written word of God. It was the most important book because it was sent to mankind and every word, jot and tittle was true because God gave it to us. He was the author. You should never say anything against the Bible. You should never challenge what it says. This was what I assumed to be correct. I was puzzled as I grew older, at the teachings of the Bible. It contained teachings we no longer followed, such as if your eye offends, you pluck it out. Also, I remember being taught that if you steal you could get your hand cut off for punishment, and if you commit adultery, you will be stoned to death. Women were considered property and men totally dominated them. Women were to be obedient to their husbands. As I grew older, I could not truly depend on my ability to trust what I heard people saying to me. Just because people said it, and just because I read it, that didn't mean I really understood – so it became a natural thing for me to challenge myself. I learned to go slow and rethink, at night before I would go to sleep, what I thought I learned that day.

This was a safeguard to make sure I got it right later in life. I would challenge the Bible and I would challenge teachers and mentors. The Bible could not talk back to me, but teachers did. They would reject my questions. As an older adult, I began asking questions and challenging concepts as I attended different churches.

Adam and Eve. Some say in the Bible, the story of Adam and Eve being cast out of the garden is myth, others say it is a metaphor. Some say it is an attempt to explain the impossible. Why do men and women do bad things to one another and kill one another? The basic concept is that after the garden, God made all children with a dual nature, of good, but also a carnal nature - and yet we are made in God's image. Therefore, it was easy to believe that all men and women are evil. It is their nature, it is their core, it is in their DNA – they have original sin.

This conservative interpretation came from a bishop of the fifth century named Augustine. He taught this theory and persuaded the church to believe it. He had a problem with sex and intercourse in his personal life. Before he became a Christian, he had a concubine and they had a son. He asked God for chastity, but "not yet." As an older man, he came to the conclusion that his earlier addiction was sinful, and sex was evil. This is one reason Christians often make intercourse and sex a sin and why it is difficult for men and women to sort out the evil from the good. I don't believe you can take the garden story as being literally true. Many do, but they mistake the first couple's disobedience to God to involve sex when it did not. The Bible says nothing like that. There is a kind, loving God who demands no conditions. Would such a God declare that sex was evil, and curse mankind with "carnal nature?" A more modern understanding of sex makes it natural and assures mankind's survival.

Becoming a Christian. What does the church require to become a Christian? My logical mind says that the dos and don'ts imposed by some churches become of primary concern and therefore become more important than the teachings of Christ. You are expected to agree with a church's theology and teachings before you can be truly admitted. Great importance is placed on creeds of the past, and unless you believe in these creeds you will not be accepted into the body of Christ. After you pass inspection and start studying the Bible and the theology of the church, you learn what is acceptable and what is not. If you challenge these mapped out beliefs, you will soon learn that you must not do that. If you proceed, you will be asked to leave the church or you will be given the silent treatment, where your "friends" in the community of believers will not talk to you.

It is sad that churches and their colleagues shun members, but they do. The rules are set in concrete and they will not move from their interpretation of God. In some ways, they are still following the rules and regulations of the medieval church, despite what we have learned since that time. Most of the things you are told you must do or cannot do, are

242

things that Jesus never taught us to believe. I believe it is up to each individual to explore what they believe as relates to their conduct and behavior.

Many churches teach different versions of believing and following God. In my own life, I believe in the teachings of Jesus and do my best to follow them. I see Jesus as a prophet, not a God, but a man like you and me.

Questions not answered. Along my spiritual journey, I had so many questions that were not answered. From reading many books on Christianity, such as those by Borg, I began to see things in a new light. I was exposed to new concepts and ideas. Here are a few of them. When you are born, you have already received the gift of the Holy Spirit, as you are never separated from God, and you already have the Holy Spirit in your heart. It is just a matter of listening and following Jesus' teachings.

I no longer believe that the Bible was written by God and that you should accept every word as being true. If you did believe that Adam and Eve passed on the carnal nature to every human being, this would mean that Mary, the mother of Jesus, had the carnal nature. And Jesus, and every like form, being exactly like man, would receive the carnal nature. I question the birth story of Jesus, but believe it is right to elevate Jesus and his teachings.

As my questions remain unanswered, I have searched out other churches and other religions, both through reading and participating. I attended the more progressive United

Church of Christ, which had a much less rigid belief system. However, even there, most did not want to hear my questioning. Thus, I attended two different Unitarian churches. I learned that some members are atheists, or humanists. They come from many church backgrounds. I attended this church as a single man, even though I was married. I was treated quite differently than if my wife had joined. I found the relationships more difficult; it was harder to make close friends. The preaching became too political for me to endure.

I have also attended Jewish services. I have read about Buddhism and Hinduism. My reading has opened my eyes to many different points of view.

CHAPTER FOUR: THREE FUNDAMENTALIST STORIES

··

I t was not only my personal spiritual journey which led me to reject many fundamentalist beliefs, but also the effect I could see it had upon those around me. I want to share three stories that affected me deeply.

Brian and his four children. I met Brian at a church party. He was passing out food and filling up people's plates. I told him I did not want any more, but he put more food on my plate and went on. This got my attention – he was so different. I was in my mid-20s and Brian was three years older than I. He had four children, three boys and a girl. I had my three children, Tim, Lynda and Ann.

We started doing things together, having meals in our homes, playing cards twice a month. He was always having fun, telling jokes. He was the jokester. He liked to be the center of attention and also a leader in the church.

Brian needed a close friend and I also needed a friend. Over the next fifty years we were inseparable. The best way to describe our relationship? He was my Roy Rogers, and I was his sidekick. In this way, he remained the center of attention with his jokes. I didn't mind. However, sometimes, he did put me down, saying little things that were hurtful. But his humor was so great that our time together was fantastic for me.

What really troubled me was seeing what was happening to his children. I watched how they dealt with the doctrine he subjected them to – that they were evil and must have a "Damascus Experience" so that they could then accept the Holy Spirit. "Road to Damascus" refers to a sudden turning point in one's life. It's in reference to the conversion to Christianity of the apostle Paul while literally on the road to Damascus from Jerusalem. Prior to that moment, he had been called Saul, and was a Pharisee who persecuted followers of Jesus.

Brian was raised by a father who was a preacher. His father was "saved" in a fundamentalist tent revival and became a preacher. Brian had two sisters and a brother. When I met Brian, he was the only one of his siblings who had this fundamentalist faith. Brian was a hardliner, teaching his children that they were fundamentalists. His wife was raised in church and was really old fashioned in her lifestyle. Brian's two boys, Joe and Bill, worked for me in the summertime when they were in high school. When he got out of high school, Bill continued working for me for a few years and then went out on his own and was financially successful as a contractor. Joe continued to work for me.

One week after Brian and I got back from a deer hunting trip, Joe was killed in a car accident. His girlfriend was killed also. Joe had rejected the church and was no longer going to church when he died. Brian and his wife handled this as well as any couple could. I had one question for Brian: "Is your son in Heaven or Hell?" Joe had rejected the church teachings, therefore to Brian, according to the teachings of the church, he was in Hell. Brian's answer to me was a wise one. "It's up to God, not me." All of the church rallied around Brian and his wife and were saying that Joe was in Heaven.

What about his other children and their faith in God? They all rejected Christianity as taught by the church. They all have had issues with depression.

I believe inside of every human being, there is a core belief about one's self: you either love yourself or hate yourself. Who are we as human beings and how does the past affect our lives?

Suicide. At the last fundamentalist church we attended, a number of members committed suicide. One was a German man who had strong ideas and feelings. He committed suicide in a nursing home with a gun. One was a middle-aged cabinet maker. According to gospel, he was committing adultery and had been convicted of tax evasion. So, he committed suicide. Another jumped off the "suicide bridge" in downtown Portland. He was middle-aged. The teenage daughter of one of the main leaders of a local fundamentalist church committed suicide. Many gays and lesbians were trying to commit suicide. The few that I know of who survived left the church. In fundamentalist churches which I attended I witnessed depression and the nervous breakdowns of three ministers.

Because of these experiences and watching others and their lives, I left the fundamentalist church and tried out different churches and studied their beliefs. I became a spiritual human, still believing there is a God and that he is guiding me in my life. And I do my best to follow the teachings of Jesus. Many of the doctrines and theologies have been formulated by man. The rules by which we live have changed over time. We all go in different directions with the different churches we attend and support.

A Salem Church of God. I was going to a friend's funeral in Salem and needed directions to the church. I pulled up their website and read something that was greatly disturbing.

It was a review of the church, which appeared right below its listing when you use the Yahoo search engine (as of 2020, it was still there.) It is a scathing commentary by a visiting family. Their middle-school aged children attended a Sunday school class. The basic lesson was that we are born evil and within our DNA there is carnal nature. In the Sunday school class, the children were given bananas to eat. They were to eat the bananas as quickly as possible. The children were mocked if they ate the bananas too politely. They were each then immediately given a large cup full of soda and told to chug it as quickly as possible. As soon as they finished, they were told it was supposed to make you throw up. They were asked how it made them feel if they didn't vomit. The bananas represented your carnal nature and that Jesus, through the Holy Spirit, was going to cleanse you and get rid of your carnal nature. When the parents were told what was taught in their Sunday school class, they were disgusted and outraged that children were being taught that they were evil from birth. No balance with the message that we are made by God in his image.

The death of one's child. Part of my church experience was observing close friends and their children, and noticing how fundamentalist teachings affected their lives.

Barry and Nancy and their children were dear friends. Barry was a professor at a college, having taught there for over thirty years. He also taught a Sunday school class for adults. He was a sociologist. He was raised on a farm in the Dakotas. He came to church every Sunday with his family, a perfectionist who lived a life of great care for his family, his church, his colleagues and his neighbors. In the summer months he would work for me in my contracting business. Later, his son Andrew worked for me too. Andrew became a business partner with another man, and they built houses in Oregon. Andrew married and divorced. He and his second wife had three children, and they were pregnant with the fourth when Andrew died in a tragic accident. Where was God? Barry and Nancy could never accept this blow. One of their daughters got pregnant out of wedlock and had to marry the father. As a result, the daughter could not afford to go to college. This was a great disappointment for Barry. The question was where was God? The theology of God having complete control of everything that happens and has a plan for your life became hard to accept.

Barry was a good man. We hunted and fished together, played cards and ate meals. He was well educated and tried to help others. He visited prisoners in jail. He worked for prison reform. He was against the death penalty. He had a rich background of religious training.

I watched Barry suffer with these teachings. He was an avid reader of religious theology and the beliefs of other churches. He left the fundamentalist church over the gay issue, as well as other issues the church taught. He chose another church, United Church of Christ, which believes all people are made in God's image, whether black or white or in the gay community. Barry believed this wholeheartedly. He worshiped there for 18 years before passing on to his reward. His other children are attending various churches. They also serve others in their community and hold leadership positions.

Barry and I had many long talks about the church and the effects of fundamentalist theology. Barry and Nancy suffered a great deal emotionally, expecting much from God and his protection over their children. What happened to their children was a great concern for him, while still wanting to please God with all his heart, mind and soul. He could not accept the death of Andrew and the teachings of the church that he was raised in. Barry influenced me a great deal, recommending books to read and discussing how to interpret the Bible and understand how it was written.

CHAPTER FIVE: HOW WE FIND THE TRUTH

....

"Imagine yourself as a living house. God comes in to rebuild that house. At first, perhaps, you can understand what He is doing. He is getting the drains right and stopping the leaks in the roof and so on; you knew that those jobs needed doing and so you are not surprised. But presently He starts knocking the house about in a way that hurts abominably and does not seem to make any sense. What on earth is He up to? The explanation is that He is building quite a different house from the one you thought of – throwing out a new wing here, putting on an extra floor there, running up towers, making court-yards. You thought you were being made into a decent little cottage: but He is building a palace. He intends to come and live in it Himself."

- "Mere Christianity," C.S. Lewis

One cannot find wisdom in absolutes. You have to live by faith and the unknown, as you cannot possibly know everything. One has to be at peace with not knowing. I have read a lot of books on theology and religious doctrine and on what each individual denomination believes. One thing is sure – churches are run by men and women. They are the ones who make the rules. The Bible was written by many different authors and in many styles, but it was written by man. Indeed, written by man and his experience with God, with the understanding and education of the time. Each individual is responsible for his or her beliefs and faith in God; the search for peace and faith is a never-ending process, because you are never going to live long enough to learn everything.

Whatever country I was born in, and whomever my parents were, whatever concept of God my parents had, whether Jewish, Christian, Muslim or atheist, I would probably embrace their teachings. I would proclaim that what I was taught was correct. I might even give my life and die for proclaiming what I believe. Because, at that time in my life, I believed it was right. I have heard Catholic clergy say, "Give me a child until he is twelve years old, and he will always be a Catholic." Whom we follow often depends on whom our parents followed – in what church and belief system we were raised.

Being human. I have raised this question before. Much of my spiritual journey has been trying to figure this out. Here I am, a physical being, just like the animals – the dogs, cats and horses. They eat food for nourishment, and they discharge their waste. So do human beings. All human beings have a soul that separates them from other animals. I am told that we are less than God, but above the animals of the world. I assumed this was right. But it is a difficult question to

254

understand. We desire to accept our physical bodies, our sex drive, our eating and discharging. We accept that we are human, mortal and going to die. I must now deal with old age and losing my physical ability to do things, which may continue to go away as I grow older. Our self-worth is built on our ability to function well. I know I have worth, but the scars, the experience over the years of hating myself, make it a struggle. My emotional life has made it a challenge to keep a balance, to stay healthy mentally and not be depressed.

Being guided. Looking back, I was poorly equipped to make the big jump from being a teenager to adulthood. I needed to survive an onslaught of my mentors telling me I missed the mark. At this time, I did have a relationship with God. I was not separated from Him. I was praying to Him, and he would guide me and help me. Yes, I had a lot of wrong ideas about girls, about the church, and about what I should do for a living. In a strange way, though, these things worked out. Did God have his hand upon me, guiding me and giving me choices that would provide me with direction and help? Providing guidance so that I could become a positive force in our society, and with people I would meet?

While in college, I wasn't sure of anything. My life seemed so mixed up, and I was so confused. Earlier in this book, I referred to a time while on a date with Gail that I felt God spoke to me. That made me feel strong and that things were going to be okay.

When I was still figuring out what I wanted to do, I believe God called on me again when he sent the three strangers to talk to me. My pastor gave me great confidence to believe that God puts together individuals who help one another, or groups of people who can bring out the best in someone, or some organization. I strongly believe that God was helping me, and in return, I was helping others.

Another time I felt God's hand on me was when I was listening to the radio while driving home from Salem and the announcer told me about Burns' book, *Feeling Good*. This was to become almost like a Bible to me. This book and my counseling helped me deal with my struggles and religious conflicts.

I have had many "Damascus Experiences" in my encounters with God and I believe that on my spiritual journey God has had his hand upon me. No one can explain these experiences otherwise. I believe with all my heart that mankind is good and that our nature is not primarily evil. I do believe that with God's help we can face the challenges in our lives.

God today. Is God not talking to us today, trying to teach us about the universe he made for us and the Mother Earth? God is teaching us how to get along with one another, to love one another. I believe God is trying to talk to us, but we aren't really listening.

My spiritual journey still continues. I have left the fundamentalist churches that were such a huge part of my life and my being for many decades. To the many friends I have left behind, I say "My God did not leave me, neither did I leave my God. He is still with me, and I am still with him."

History cautions us to not accept everything the church says. Former President Jimmy Carter left his church because women were not being allowed to become leaders. The church taught that women are to be quiet, to go home and talk to their husbands if they have any questions. In many churches women still cannot be a minister or priest.

Slavery is still taught in a few churches today. Most churches in the South used religion to support slavery throughout the 1800s. Stonewall Jackson started the Democratic Party, and for over 100 years they supported slavery or legislation that kept African Americans from voting.

Some religious leaders feel an obligation to ask the congregation to vote or support their candidates. In the 1930s, some priests and ministers supported the Nazis. After the Allies won the war, they helped some Nazis escape to foreign countries. In Germany they had taken away the citizens' guns, eliminating the ability of Jews to defend themselves. Over six million Jews were killed. Priests and pastors should not show any bias toward political candidates. They could be wrong.

I do not believe in dualism: that you are made in God's image but at the same time, evil is in every person. I do not believe sex is evil. I accept the gay and lesbian community as being a product of God. Matthew Fox's book *Original Blessings* supports my view that we are made in God's image and that we should not believe in dual nature. I recommend this book.

I now call God the power of the universe, as we take in how large this space is. Just think of a loving God, who offers unconditional love. I have water to drink, food to eat, outstanding shelter to live in, wonderful friends, wonderful children and a wonderful wife. Life is good.

We have been set free to pursue happiness as best we can and certainly the teachings of Jesus can help us. I think the Jewish faith has much to be admired, by recognizing Jesus as a prophet, not a Savior.

One of the wonderful things for me is that, because I no longer attend churches that muddle my feelings about God, I now experience no depression to speak of. Have you ever prayed to God to give you new ideas and new thoughts? I have asked God to give me new ideas and new thoughts about who I am, and who He is, and what to expect from God. I have asked Him what I am to do with my remaining time on earth.

I am listening, and I believe I am getting answers.

EPILOGUE

....

The winter of my life has brought the joy of winning.

Aunt Bessie was right – I am a "good little boy." I have value.

Fortunately, I was not killed when I was born a blue baby.

My God is a creative God of the universe. My God is a God of unconditional love, of acceptance, of approval of all mankind. You can self-talk and stand up to the battles in your mind.

Here are some of the things I did to win the battle: I was a plow horse of value; slow but true. I gave myself time. I can be successful if you give me time.

I forgave others and myself. I have no college degree; I am largely self-taught.

I learned that it is all right not to have all the answers. The answer is blowing in the wind. The Bible is an ancient book. It was written to try and explain the unexplainable. It is old science. It was old men seeking answers in their time. It does have a great deal of wisdom. The teachings of Jesus will bring success and love to your life.

Is It All Right to be Human?

The sweet taste of success: My accomplishments are ever before me. I accomplished the impossible.

ACKNOWLEDGEMENTS

....

Many have assisted me in getting this manuscript ready for publication. A special thank you to:

My wife Gail

Robert Wm. Davis

David Johnson, organizing and editing

My children for reviewing portions of the manuscript

Howard Neal, technical and computer assistance

My brother Mike Burroughs – for his encouragement and financial assistance to publishing

Rose O'Reilly Hoisington, my illustrator

Nancy Nolan, my editor

APPENDIX A: SUGGESTED READING

······································

When Bad Things Happen to Good People, Rabbi Harold S. Kushner

Rescuing the Bible from Fundamentalism: A Bishop Rethinks the Meaning of Scripture, Bishop John Shelby Spong

Meeting Jesus Again for the First Time: The Historical Jesus and the Heart of Contemporary Faith; The Heart of Christianity; Jesus, Marcus J. Borg

Saving Jesus from Church: How to Stop Worshiping Christ and Start Following Jesus, Rev. Robin R. Meyers

Jesus Before the Gospels: How the Earliest Christians Remembered, Changed and Invented Their Stories of the Savior, Bart D. Ehrman

The Gifts of Imperfection; Daring Greatly; Braving the Wilderness, Brené Brown

Transforming Anxiety, Doc Childre & Deborah Rozman

Feeling Good – the New Mood Therapy, by David D. Burns.

Happier, Tal Ben-Shahar

Buddhism Plain and Simple : The Practice of Being Aware, Right Now, Every Day, Steve Hagen

Is It All Right to be Human?

Brain Lock – Free Yourself from Obsessive-Compulsive Behavior,
Jeffrey M. Schwartz

*You Can Handle It: Ten Steps to Shift Stress from Problem to
Possibility,* Margaret Wehrenberg

A Little History of Religion, Richard Holloway

Original Blessings, Matthew Fox

Chuck and Gail with Logan, Nikhil, Owen and Avi

Nikhil, Owen Gail, Logan and Chuck

On the Oregon coast

42nd wedding anniversary celebration

Working together, as always

In Florida on a cross-country trip

Richmond Church of God basketball team (Chuck far left, top)

Holladay Park Church of God team

Together 24/7

50th Wedding Anniversary

Chuck and Don

Fishing - Owen and Chuck

Chuck and Jared

On the slopes of Mt. Hood

Above: Tim, Ann and Lynda;
below, Chuck with Ann

Above: Chuck with Lynda
Below: Skiing with Tim

APPENDIX B: GRATITUDE FROM FRIENDS

···

Dear Chuck and Gail:

Thank you guys for the card and your support throughout the years. If it wasn't for working on your garden, I don't know if I'd be majoring in what I am today, Agriculture and Environmental Science. I don't know if I would've gotten the seed planted for what I wanted to do with my life. With this quarantine, I've even started my first garden on my own with carrots, beans, squash, cucumbers and tomatoes. And many more things on the way. Thank you guys for everything you have given me.

- Love, Jared

Your note was so gracious and encouraging. Thanks Chuck, for being my "Winter Friend", and also through the many years you kept me grounded and "prepared" while I was spontaneous. Thanks again for "Friendship" and your excellent note.

- Friends forever, Don and Mary

Thank you for inviting us to this wonderful (anniversary) event. We appreciate all the work you do for our neighborhood youth and for our community.

- All the best, Ray and Tina

Thank you for inviting us into your home and giving us an opportunity to meet your friends and neighbors. We had a wonderful time. Thank you for all the good things you do for our community.

- Best, Melanie, Ilya and Gabe

Thank you for everything you have done for our neighborhood by helping with the mailbox project! I never thought we would be able to move them. God moves mountains and Chuck moves mountains, too! Thank you for sharing how God is using your message to encourage people in the park of Happy Valley. You have an inspiring life story. I hope you will write it down for your grandchildren.

- Very respectfully, Rachel

Happy New Year to you! We wish you many wonderful moments – health, hope, love. We appreciate watching your lives and how you give to family and to the community (particularly to the four boys.) You are very special neighbors, for sure! Which brings me to the subject of quilts! The quilt is a creative "Labor of Love." Thank you so much for your gift! It is beautifully made, a treasure, and will be a joy to us for years to come. Wonderful!

- With much appreciation, Shirley and Irv

I think of you so often and all the love and goodness you have shared with Owen and the kids of Happy Valley. Thank you, thank you, thank you. It is such a crazy world right now. But, my son and his parents know two lights in the fog, you two! You HAVE been (and will be) a light in Owen's life.

- With deep and sincere appreciation, Margo

Chuck Burroughs was born on August 2, 1939 in the small town of Franklin, Ohio. He was one of three boys born to a hard-working but strict father and kind but meek mother. Chuck was born with learning disabilities which made school challenging, but he excelled in sports, particularly basketball. Immersed in the teachings of the very conservative Church of God, Chuck began to doubt his faith and his ability to live up to an unforgiving standard of goodness, which caused him severe emotional challenges. Eventually, Chuck taught himself to read, and he graduated from high school and attended college at Warner Pacific College in Oregon in the early 1960s. He held a number of jobs, finally opening his own successful construction business, which he headed for 45 years. Chuck married Gail Hanson in 1962, and they had three children, Tim, Lynda and Ann. They now have 13 grandchildren and 11 great-grandchildren, with two more on the way. Chuck has worked hard to overcome Obsessive-Compulsive Disorder anxiety, and depression, and recently compiled a packet of educational materials about these disabilities and how to confront them to share with others who might benefit.

Married for 59 years, Chuck and Gail reside in Happy Valley, Oregon. This memoir is Chuck's first book.

To request additional material, including Chuck's Packet of Resources; a version of Chuck's relaxation tape; or to see a video of Chuck and Gail's 50th wedding anniversary party, contact Nolan Kerr Press at info@nolankerr.com. You can also visit Chuck's web site and blog at www.chuckburroughs.net. Visit www.Amazon.com to purchase additional copies of the book. If you enjoyed reading *Is It All Right to be Human?*, consider reviewing it on Amazon!